HAVERFORDWEST
MY GRANDSTAND

BILL RICHARDS

Cover Picture: From a post card, circa 1908, showing suffragettes meeting at the Castle Square, with familiar Haverfordwest buildings in the background. (From the Gerald Oliver Collection).

ISBN No. 0 9517540 3 3
Published by Haverfordwest Civic Society © 1994
Printed by Withybush Printers Ltd.

Primitive watercolour of Hill Street, Haverfordwest, circa 1870
Courtesy: Anthony Morris, Esq.

CONTENTS

CHAPTER		PAGE
	INTRODUCTION	4
	AUTHOR'S NOTE	5
1	WILLINGLY TO SCHOOL	7
2	HEIGH-HO, HEIGH-HO	12
3	WORKHOUSE DAYS	18
4	ON TOUR WITH GWILYM	22
5	THE GRAMMAR SCHOOL ROW	26
I	PICTURE GALLERY I	30
6	PROSPERITY COMES TO THE COUNTRYSIDE	39
7	WINNERS AND LOSERS	44
8	TURBULENT YEARS	49
9	SPREADING THE NEWS (1)	57
10	SPREADING THE NEWS (2)	64
II	PICTURE GALLERY II	72
11	TOO LITTLE, TOO LATE	83
12	THE SHIRE HALL	87
13	THE ASSIZES AND QUARTER SESSIONS	94
14	THE LIGHTER SIDE	105
15	AN UNCROWNED KING	112
III	PICTURE GALLERY III	118
16	ANY ADVANCE ON TWO HUNDRED	124
17	A VICTORIAN RECORD	131
18	ALL SAID AND DONE	137

INTRODUCTION

"Haverfordwest My Grandstand" is a parade of local personalities which also includes a vast amount of information on many of the events, organisations and institutions which have helped over the years to make Haverfordwest a town of unusual distinction. The photographs are of people rather than of places. The author touches briefly on his country boyhood before going on to deal with his experiences as a reporter for the "West Wales Guardian," first as a wide-eyed junior doing the Haverfordwest news round and then covering the county political scene from early Gwilym Lloyd George to late Desmond Donnelly, a turbulent period in the Pembrokeshire story. He also deals with the far-reaching developments in local government, including a description of how Pembrokeshire lost the battle for its independence, and deplores the drastic changes in the administration of the law, in particular the loss of the ancient Courts of Assize and Quarter Sessions. At the same time he shows there is a light-hearted side, even to the law. The Shire Hall, the venue for Haverfordwest's important civic and other events, is described in some detail while the author also tells a fascinating story of the development of the two county newspapers, the "Guardian" and the "Telegraph", and the unique relationship between the two proprietors, Joseph William Hammond and John Thomas, both dedicated newspapermen but so different in character.

A third old business which receives a deserved tribute here is that of R.K. Lucas & Son, Estate Agents, which has been operating in Haverfordwest under one name or another for about two hundred years, and the book quotes in full an unusual old document about Haverfordwest charities, including the Freemen and their Portfield inheritance, with references to the origins of Portfield Fair. Haverfordians will also surely read with great interest the details of the long and extraordinary row which followed the dismissal of five Grammar School masters in the early 1930's.

"Haverfordwest My Grandstand" is wide-ranging, informative and good humoured, and it ensures that many interesting and unique aspects of local history are placed on permanent record.

Gerald Oliver
Chairman
Haverfordwest Civic Society

AUTHOR'S NOTE

"Haverfordwest My Grandstand" is an amalgam of reminiscence and researched local history based on over fifty years experience as a Pembrokeshire newspaper reporter and recorded in no particular order. Some of the material has appeared previously as part of my work for the "West Wales Guardian". The reminiscence is necessarily personal and I hope the reader will forgive the use of the personal pronoun - kept to a minimum - in the realisation that to try and avoid it completely in such circumstances would be less acceptable than its judicious use. As far as the research is concerned my salvation, once again, was the Haverfordwest Record Office where the staff, under the Dyfed County Archivist, Mr. John Owen, fully maintained a now well known reputation for helpfulness. I consulted the old files of the two County newspapers, the "Telegraph" and "Guardian", referred to Douglas James' invaluable "Haverfordwest and its Story", read an ancient and unattributed booklet on the Haverfordwest Charities and, as far as Chapter Nine (the history of the "Telegraph") is concerned, benefited greatly from information gained during many delightful conversations over the years with Mrs. Constance Lloyd, J.P. widow of John Thomas, the man who in the nineteen twenties and thirties laid the foundations of the "Western Telegraph", now Wales' leading weekly newspaper.

Mr. Paul Lucas co-operated most willingly in the research into the history of R.K. Lucas & Son, the remarkable firm of which he is now a principal, and a great many other people helped in various ways, including the provision of photographs of several of the personalities dealt with herein. For such help I express sincere gratitude.

Once again I am indebted to Haverfordwest Civic Society, especially its chairman, Mr. Gerald Oliver, honorary secretary, Mr. Maldwyn Thomas, and financial secretary, Mr. R. C. Livesey, for their encouragement and valued advice on several aspects of this undertaking. To have accepted a second book from my pen within a few years required a special kind of friendship and courage, of which I am deeply appreciative.

Grateful thanks are also expressed to the following who generously made contributions towards the cost of producing this book:- Haverfordwest Gild of Freemen; Messrs. B.H. Munt & Sons; Messrs R.K. Lucas & Son; Haverfordwest Town Council; Peter Richards, Esq. (Bridgend); and to the Cultural Services Department of Dyfed County Council for their assistance.

November 1994

Copies of "Haverfordwest My Grandstand" by Bill Richards may be obtained from Maldwyn Thomas, Hon. Secretary, Haverfordwest Civic Society, 31, Dunsany Park, Haverfordwest, Pembrokeshire, SA61 1UD. Price £7 inclusive of postage and packaging. (Cheques should be made out in favour of Haverfordwest Civic Society).

CHAPTER ONE

WILLINGLY TO SCHOOL

I remember everything as if it were yesterday
- Maurice Chevalier in "Gigi"

I remember everything too - boyhood dreams, youthful ambitions and the growing realisation that life is just a patchwork of good and evil and that homo sapiens is the most complex, calculating, devious and selfish of all God's creatures yet is capable of the most extraordinary self sacrifice.

Boyhood for me was the nineteen twenties when David Lloyd George's land fit for heroes had already turned into a land of unemployment and near starvation. Lloyd George's famous Coalition had gone and the great man himself was in the political wilderness. I remember a cartoon in a national newspaper showing David Lloyd George sitting alone on a five-barred gate at night with a sour-faced man in the moon looking down, and underneath was the caption "All By Yourself in The Moonlight" - the title of a popular song of the twenties. But in the Keyston - Camrose area, where I was brought up, Lloyd George was still the man who won the war, the people's friend and, therefore, a great hero. Did I say a hero? He was more than that. He was a god. The whole area was solid Lloyd George Liberal. Children were named after him. If someone was in receipt of benefit under the 1911 National Insurance Act they were said to be "under Lloyd George" because he was largely responsible for that important legislation. This expression sometimes produced sly chuckles if a female were involved, though I was not supposed to know what it meant and certainly Lloyd George's amorous proclivities which hit the headlines many years later were generally unknown then. He was a man beyond suspicion. His picture hung in every front room. In our own parlour I remember a framed Temperance Society Certificate which bore the photographs of five great war leaders, all of whom, it was claimed, had renounced the demon drink. Lloyd George was one of them. We didn't know then that he loved his Irish whiskey!

One of the great events of my early life was going with my father to Milford Haven - quite an adventure at that time - where David Lloyd

George was addressing an open air meeting in the field upon which the Central Secondary School was subsequently built. We stood on the edge of the huge crowd but I managed to catch a glimpse of the famous white locks. Gwilym Lloyd George, then Pembrokeshire's M.P., presided and I remember him saying "I'm sure you haven't all come here to listen to me, so I have great pleasure in introducing to you Mr.David Lloyd George". I wondered why he didn't just say "my father".

I remember the twenties for long hot summers, hard winters and the grinding poverty which kept the countryside subdued. To me, boyhood was fetching and carrying on the farm, playing in the fields, expeditions into nearby woodlands, climbing trees, bird nesting, running, jumping, racing - on legs which never tired and did not grow much either. School was never a chore. Far from it. It was just that school was nearly three miles away from my home and from the age of five I had to leg it twice a day, rain or shine, come hell or high water. When it rained, which was often, we got wet through and the school fires (coal, of course) were obscured for hours by children's clothing drying off on the guard rails, sending up clouds of steam. School meals had not even been thought of then and all the children carried sandwiches, mostly bread and jam, which we ate in the playground or, if it was very wet, at our desks. A few local families were so poor that their children came to school in ragged jerseys, corduroy trousers, leaky boots and sometimes not any food at all. Deep ploughs the share by poverty depressed! But they never went hungry, thanks to a great-hearted headmaster, Mr.R.T. Griffiths, who brought in plates heaped with bread and jam from the adjoining schoolhouse. Mr.Griffiths, a member of the well-known Griffiths family of City Road Garage, Haverfordwest, was a most able man, loved by everyone, and it was a great loss to the whole district when after twenty one years at Camrose South School he left to become headmaster at Hakin.

These then were the "good old days" of the twenties in the Pembrokeshire countryside. I'm sure that most of those who lived through those times find it hard to resist a wry smile at all the fuss that is made nowadays about school transport, school meals, the treatment of backward children, child psychology etc, etc, and so on. I do not applaud those hard times, of course, but most of my generation survived with amazing resilience and in good health - and, looking back, I am so thankful that I went to school when hard work was the norm and education was in no way optional! To a large extent we had to make our own amusement. Popular radio had not yet arrived and the gramophone was too expensive. In our home we were lucky to have a harmonium which my mother loved to play and sometimes the family would gather round and give Sankey the full treatment for an hour or so. Mostly, though, it was reading and playing cards and draughts, and on Sundays it was off to chapel, three times or else! There were occasional village concerts where people who thought they had talent sang songs, recited or did little sketches, sometimes with blackened faces. Popular "artistes" included Ivor Lewis, Haverfordwest who sang songs like "The Sheik of Araby," "Riding On A Camel In The Desert," and "Excelsior" to tremendous effect; Mr.Ross, the Haverfordwest electrical dealer who was a good conjurer; Mr. Phil. Hancock, Camrose; and Mr.Jack Marr of Robleson, Camrose, a fine baritone. Mr.Ross's tricks were soon forgotten but everyone remembered that he had a Morris car with a plate affixed to the back bearing the message "If You Can Read This You Are Too Damned Near". This was regarded as very daring at that time and Mr.Ross was written down as a bit of a lad!

I also remember people being greatly impressed when Gwilym Davies, a local young man billed to sing a solo at a packed concert at the tiny village hall at Nolton, stepped on to the platform and began "Tout seul a' la lune" and proceeded to sing the whole of "All By Yourself In The Moonlight" in French! It created a tremendous impression, if slightly off key, and the locals wondered for weeks where Gwilym had learned all that French!

People thought nothing of walking three of four miles to attend a concert or chapel anniversary. There was no other form of transport in that part of the countryside, apart from the occasional bicycle. Doctor the Rev. Roderick Michael (Haverfordwest and later of Birmingham) used to say in one of his popular sermons "man could travel no faster than a horse could gallop" - not strictly true, of course, but it had a ring to it!

First cars in our district were owned by Mr.Dick Wade (later to be widely known as Alderman R.S. Wade, a leading county figure), Mr.Tom Owen, Pelcomb Cross and, nearer to my home, his brother Mr.Reesy Owen of Summerhill, who also became a well known public man. Mr.Reesy Owen's car was an Angus Sanderson, my main memory of which was that it broke down with distressing regularity. Mr.Owen also had the distinction of being the only farmer in the district to own a tractor - a Fordson, on the seat of which I sat in trembling excitement on many occasions, my legs still well short of the clutch and brake pedals. My tractor driving ambitions greatly amused Reesy Owen, a kindly and learned man whose influence for good in all sorts of ways is still remembered with gratitude in the district.

Another early motorist in the district was the Rev. David Garro Jones, the noted pastor of Keyston Congregational Chapel. As I related in my book "Lives of Great Men", (a history of Keyston Chapel), Garro was well over sixty when he acquired a bull-nosed Morris two seater (with dickey!) and learned to drive with boyish enthusiasm. Soon he was careering along the country lanes at reckless speeds, waving flamboyantly to everyone he saw and frequently veering to the wrong side in doing so! As his daughter, Mrs Edith Thomas, commented "Only those who were brave enough to accept a lift with him could fully appreciate the thrills of the road". Garro was a great character, a pastor-extraordinaire and an ingenious fund-raiser and worker for his church. His four-year ministry at Keyston enriched the quality of local life.

A momentous family event occurred in the mid-twenties when my father, after long and anxious consideration, acquired a brand new Model T Ford for use in his business as a farmer and rabbit and game dealer. The locals watched my father's progress as a motorist with tremendous interest because he was already over fifty and, what was more, had lost a leg in a farm accident many years before which, of course, added greatly to the difficulties of a new driver. But the old man was nothing if not courageous and soon be was chugging along the country lanes, highly delighted at the luxury and speed of his new acquisition compared with the previously used horse and trap. It was lucky for him there was no driving test in those days! The Model T was an extraordinary motor.

Thanks to my father's indulgence, I had my first driving lessons in it - at an age when I could scarcely see over the steering wheel! - so I am not likely to forget its many peculiar features. It stood high off the ground and the inside controls were stark and minimal - a high steering wheel, the bars of which curved away from the driver, and throttle and ignition levers on ratchets on the steering column; a handbrake and three pedals, which were the clutch, footbrake and reverse gear. To start the car one had to turn on the ignition switch on the dashboard and then get out and swing the fixed starting handle, risking a broken arm if it "kicked". The choke was a wire which came out looped alongside the starting handle. There was no self-starter. Once the engine was running the driver got moving by releasing the handbrake to its half-way mark and pressing the clutch pedal. This engaged low gear. The driver then revved-up to about 15 mph (using the hand throttle, of course, there being no accelerator) and, after pushing the handbrake fully forward he took his foot off the clutch - and lo! he was in top! These were the two forward gears. Reverse was obtained by pressing the third pedal mentioned above! After many years of reliable service, the old Ford began to deteriorate and when it was reaching the end of its usefulness the mudguards became rusty and needed replacement, a fact which did not escape the eagle eye of our friendly local bobby, P.C. Fred James (later Sergeant). My father ignored his repeated warnings and eventually received a summons for using the vehicle without proper mudguards. He wrote to the court pleading guilty, apologising and saying "I have a pair of wings at home, but haven't had time to fix them on". In reporting this, the "Evening Post" newspaper (Swansea) added the comment "We wonder if he had a golden harp as well". The family fell about but for some reason father, normally so good humoured, was furious and threatened to "take that newspaper to court". However, he cooled down and even managed a smile when we pointed out that the newspaper gave his age as forty five when he was by then over sixty.

In the late autumn of 1929 I made my first ever visit to the "Guardian" office in Market Street, Haverfordwest and there I was interviewed by a small, wiry gentleman with a ruddy complexion and white hair - Mr.J.W. Hammond, the owner and editor. After a few minutes conversation he told me he was prepared to take me on as a trainee reporter, adding rather severely "But remember, it is strictly on a month's trial". At the end of the month I waited full of trepidation but the brusque Mr.Hammond said nothing and I sat tight. In the event, the matter was never mentioned again and, full-time and part-time, the "month's trial" went on for over sixty years!

CHAPTER TWO

HEIGH - HO, HEIGH - HO

> If you see a man about half shabby with dandruff on his collar, an eye like a gimlet, smoking cut plug, and knowing more than J.P. Morgan and Shakespeare put together if that man ain't a reporter I never saw one .
> -O.Henry

A junior reporter's life in the early thirties wasn't all beer and skittles. Mostly it was pretty hard graft. There were numerous routine calls (on foot, not by telephone) and office work in the daytime, followed by endless meetings and social events in the evenings. Everything had to be written up straightaway for the printers. We had no office hours outside the twenty-four! On Saturdays there was the inevitable football match or, in the summer months, sports meeting. Reporters attended about everything that was held, regardless of the day, the hour or the news value. The press conference had not been invented. There was no such thing as a hand-out. In what spare time was available, we wrestled with the fiendish intricacies devised by Sir Isaac Pitman, the shorthand pioneer.

Haverfordwest was to be my grandstand for Pembrokeshire's passing show, a phantasmagoria of endless fascination, and my very first reporting assignment was an eisteddfod at Ford Chapel, Wolfscastle - on a Whit Monday! How I got there I don't remember but I cannot forget that late that night, filled to the gills with music and poetry, I walked, yes walked, most of the way back to Haverfordwest, accompanied by fellow-scribe Sylvan Howell of the "Western Telegraph," later to become a prominent Welsh journalist. That walk established a life-long friendship, but little did either of us think then that we would both eventually become presiding magistrates at the Petty Sessional Courts of Cardigan and Haverfordwest respectively.

One day a week I spent covering Haverfordwest local news. This entailed walking round the town (sometimes several times) to call on all the preachers, parsons, and "newsy persons" in the hope that they would supply a few news paragraphs, known then and now as "Harfat pars". Canon T.O. Phillips, vicar of St. Mary's and a huge man with a kindly face, would come to the door and always say the same thing - "Ah good morning the 'Guardian' no nothing today good morning" without pausing for breath, and I was on my way, notebook intact. I had better luck with Rev. W.J. Thomas, Bethesda, who usually served up a few snippets, and better luck still with Rev. W.H. Williams, Hill Park, who could reel off a third of a column of pars without any trouble at all, thus saving my bacon on many a quiet day. Mr. Williams was a splendid man in every respect and he surprised me one day by asking if he could be paid for his contributions. I put the matter to Mr. Hammond who, as usual, had a quick and short answer. "Tell Mr.Williams he is lucky we don't charge him for advertising his chapel" he said. I relayed this to Mr. Williams and no more was heard on the subject.

Rev. Nicholson Jones, Tabernacle, was nothing like so prolific as Rev. Williams, but he was easily the most meticulous of the news-givers. As related in my history of the Tabernacle "A Well-Found Ship," he would first make sure that you were seated comfortably and he would say "Now my boy, get out your notebook" and then, hands folded over his ample abdomen, he would dictate slowly, saying "capital letter", "comma", "full stop", etc in all the appropriate places. Then, inevitably, it was "Now, my boy, read that back to me," which was something of a strain having regard to my elementary shorthand, but splendid training nevertheless. Rev. Nicholson Jones' paragraphs were gems of composition which I shamelessly passed off as my own, and the editor thought I was improving. I could make no progress at all with Rev. Baring Gould, vicar of St. Martins. He would poke his head round the Vicarage door and say in reply to my stock question "News? What news do you think I've got?" and close the door again. He was a man greatly venerated in Haverfordwest and I'm sure he never intended to be unkind, but his attitude to me was so off-hand that I soon crossed him off my calling list.

Rev. W.J. Williams, St. Thomas, was more helpful, though not a great paragraph provider. What I shall never forget about him was that when he left Haverfordwest for Saundersfoot his parishioners presented him with a seven-day clock, and a local newspaper, reporting the event, made a printer's error in describing the gift, dropping one vital letter. When I next called on Rev. Nicholson Jones he said casually "I read about the presentation to Rev. Williams," paused, and then added with only the hint of a twinkle in his eyes "I've never heard of a seven-day one before".

For many years after that classic misprint the local newspapers, for safety's sake, never referred to "a clock". It was always "a timepiece".

On Thursday nights between ten and eleven it was my duty to dash round the Haverfordwest billiard halls to get the results of all the Milford and District Billiards League matches. Billiards and snooker were extremely popular in those days and match results and league tables were followed with great interest in the "Guardian". I usually had five halls to visit - the Liberal Club, St. Mary's Institute, Hill Lane Institute, Workingmen's Club (behind the County Hotel, then the Salutation) and the Balfour. It wasn't an easy assignment because if I arrived early the match hadn't finished, and if late the club would be closed for the night, everyone gone home, and of course, it was vital to get the results that night in time for inclusion in the next day's "Guardian". Every week I extracted solemn promises from a variety of characters that they would keep the results until I arrived but this seldom happened. If only they had realised the heartbreak. . . . . !

Reporters also attended church and chapel teas to get the names of the persons involved, and even stayed for the entertainment which usually followed. I still have vivid memories of St. Mary's annual tea and concert in the church hall when the programme was supplied by artistes like Mrs Annie Baggott, Madame Bishop, and Mr.W.S. Brewer singing excerpts from the "Mikado" with tremendous verve. Many a trio was performed with brio! The programme was always held together by Mr. Griffin Bishop and his orchestra who, over the years, made an incalculable contribution to the musical life and culture of Haverfordwest. I remember the nostalgia produced by the singing of "After The Ball Is Over" which was an old, old favourite even in those far-off days.

Another duty which gave me particular pleasure was reporting amateur dramatics in Haverfordwest. Those were the days of The Community Players, a company of enthusiasts who blazed a trail in local drama production. Under the leadership of experienced people like Mr. Bill Eynon and Mr. Eber Cox, the Community Players put on many a first-class play at the Palace Theatre which was filled for every performance. As Mr. Eynon and Mr. Cox both lived in City Road, within a few doors of my lodgings, I became closely involved with the Community Players and was soon regarded as their unofficial press officer, a pleasant office indeed! When they produced "The Passing of the Third Floor Back" I was completely enthralled and my piece for the paper ran easily from my pen which, to put it mildly, was a new experience! The next day, the chief reporter, John Higgins, a dour Scotsman and hard taskmaster if ever there was one, called me aside and said "I liked your report of the play. If you stick at it and study the 'Sunday Observer' you could do well". It was the very first word of encouragement I had heard him utter. So I valued it, stuck at the job and read the "Sunday Observer".

When I started in journalism there was an established way of life which apparently would never change. Re-organisation in Government, Local Government and the social structure, as far as we knew, had never been considered, even by officialdom who had yet to achieve the power and proliferation which we were soon to know. The system of education - the elementary school, then the grammar school and, for a few, college or university - seemed as safe as the Bank of England. Pleasures were simple because there was no money about. Another war was not a serious possibility; a siren was still a beautiful woman and when a man put the lights out it wasn't to watch television.

Through my newspaper work I soon became engrossed in local activities, especially in connection with the Councils and the Courts. This period saw the election of the first woman member of Haverfordwest Borough Council, Mrs A.V.A. Lloyd of Bush Row, followed a month later at a by-election, by the second, Mrs Mary Thomas, Wilton House. Mrs Thomas went on to become the first woman Mayor and Admiral of the Port in 1940-41. Dominating the Haverfordwest Borough Council were those two outstanding public men, Aldermen J.W. Hammond and L.H. Ellis. It was through their persistent efforts against great odds that the Parade Recreation Ground was eventually established. They also fought hard for such things as a Haverfordwest swimming pool and a worthwhile scheme for the Market Hall but were spragged by the recalcitrants on the Council who were petrified at the possibility of losing votes because of public expenditure. Almost single-handed, Alderman Hammond campaigned for years for a car park "behind" High Street and for a civic centre at Prospect Place providing offices for all the central and local government services in the area. Both schemes were described at the time as "impossible" or "too expensive" or just "pie in the sky". But today the car park in Castle Lake is a great boon to Haverfordwest. The civic centre would also have become a reality but for the obstruction of one authority, Haverfordwest Rural District Council. The scheme had reached the stage where all of the authorities had agreed to it in principle - except Haverfordwest RDC, whose "No" put an end to it. No doubt the RDC already had in mind its own concrete monster which it proceeded to build some years later and which now rejoices in the name of Cambria House.

Both Alderman Hammond and Alderman Ellis were much criticised for their progressive views but both philosophically accepted this as part of public life and were not easily put off. Alderman Ellis was also an organiser of exceptional ability. Carnivals, fetes, boxing tourneys, football matches, dances - Leslie Ellis organised all these for good causes and raised thousands of pounds, particularly for the old County War Memorial Hospital. The carnivals of the early thirties have never been beaten for size, originality and colour, not to mention enthusiasm! But even in this connection The Big Promoter, as he became known, was criticised, although the criticisms were mainly reserved for his absence and were made by people who envied his ability.

At county level, I remember Sir Evan D. Jones, then the Lord Lieutenant, as a meticulous public speaker; Baron de Rutzen who was always sparring lightheartedly (verbally) with the more serious-minded Lord Merthyr: and Alderman G.S. Kelway, the terror of the County Council and its staff. The genial Baron, who often walked around Haverfordwest in old clothes and with a knobbly stick across his shoulder, was chief guest at a Haverfordwest Grammar School speech day in the early thirties. The speech day at that time was a long and solemn occasion when serious advice about their conduct and future life was offered by the speaker to the boys, who usually went home in a pretty glum mood. But for once, anyway, the Baron changed all that. To everybody's amazement, he advised the boys to drink beer when they grew up! "Keep off the spirits - whisky will rot your gut" he told them. "If you stick to beer you won't go far wrong". This might sound like wise advice today but in the narrow-minded, disciplinarian early thirties it was sensational. The boys were delighted but many adults shook their heads and wondered what on earth things were coming to!

When I began reporting County Council committee meetings my senior colleague, Lloyd Phillips, told me "If Alderman Kelway says anything, make a note of it. He is always right". I thought this must be a little exaggerated but soon found it to be accurate advice. It was Alderman Kelway who, when asked "How many are working in the County Offices now?" replied without hesitation "About half of them". He was a first-class public man, acutely intelligent, utterly fearless and genuinely interested in public work. He was gruff of manner and far from popular, but was liked by those who knew him. I remember attending a lavish banquet at the Fishguard Bay Hotel given by Alderman A. Owen Williams, St. Davids, to mark the Coronation of King George VI which occurred during his chairmanship of the County Council. There were nearly a dozen toasts (this was the average in those days) one of which was proposed by Mr.Gil Jones, a noted speaker and Milford personality, who summed up the position respecting the County Council in one sentence. "When I get home on Friday nights" said Mr. Jones, "I open the 'Guardian' and read the reports of the County Council and do you know - when I go down the column and mark off the number of times 'Lord Merthyr said' and then the number of times 'Alderman Kelway said' by the time I reach the bottom I have to sharpen my pencil". Only two other things I remember about that banquet. A North Pembrokeshire schoolmaster got drunk and made a fool of himself in front of his employers, and one of the best speeches of the evening was made by a local journalist, Mr. W.J. Emmerson, responding to the very last toast, that to 'The Press.' Bill Emmerson hailed from Pembroke Dock, went to Haverfordwest Grammar School and, after serving a journalistic apprenticeship on the 'Guardian' at Haverfordwest, moved to Fishguard where he became one of the best known personalities in North Pembrokeshire.

Banquets were not so frequent then as they were to become. But they were far more elaborate. There were long toast lists involving many speakers and the speeches went on for hour after hour while the guests steadily got the worse for wear. At a great banquet at Milford Haven to celebrate the inauguration of the Precelly water scheme the speeches went on and on, and some became lyrical about 'turning our eyes to the hills' etc. When it came his turn to speak, Milford's well-remembered medical officer, Dr. H.O. Williams, commented "You're all praising Precelly water today but I notice that not many of you are drinking it". One of Milford's wittiest men, in public and private, was Mr. Arthur Codd. A ship's chandler, he was prominent for years in Milford affairs, a star man always surrounded by friends. Then suddenly he was crippled by ill-health. When I was covering Milford Haven news for the "Guardian" during the last war, I sometimes saw him moving slowly along the street on his stick, a sad, lonely figure. How cruel fate can be! One of Arthur Codd's best remembered remarks was made at an open-air social function in Milford Haven, when a local personality, inebriated as usual, staggered up to a small group of ladies and gentlemen and demanded loudly "Where can I have a . . . . . ?" Like lightning Mr.Codd replied "Go along there and turn left and you'll see the sign 'Gentlemen' - but don't let that stop you".

CHAPTER THREE

WORKHOUSE DAYS

> Journalism, a good mistress
> But a poor wife.
> - *Rudyard Kipling*

The first meetings of Haverfordwest Rural District Council which I attended were held at Priory Mount, the local workhouse. Members were allowed the use of a large, bare room with a stone floor and sat at an oblong table, at the top end of which was a dais for the chairman and clerk. The reporters sat on the bottom ledge of the dais, literally at the chairman's feet, notebooks resting on their knees. At my very first meeting I was surprised to find that one of the men on the dais did practically all the talking. I concluded that he must be the chairman but, on inquiring, found that he was, in fact, the clerk, Mr. Walter Evans. The meetings, I was soon to learn, were almost completely dominated by the clerk. I did not get to know Mr. Walter Evans well - he never deigned to have much to do with junior pressmen - but it was obvious that he had influence over the R.D.C. and as the Council covered nearly half the county that influence was considerable. Of course, the Haverfordwest R.D.C. of the twenties and thirties was a mere babe compared with the giant it was to become after the war. Mr. Walter Evans was only a part-time clerk and apart from two sanitary inspectors, a part-time medical officer, a rating officer and one or two clerical assistants had no large supporting staff. Who at that time could have foreseen that in little more than ten years the R.D.C. would be undertaking schemes costing hundreds of thousands of pounds under the direction of various departments all heavily and expensively staffed? It was a far cry from 1894 when the R.D.C. was set up to succeed Haverfordwest Poor Law Union, carrying out the functions of a sanitary authority and also with responsibility for local highways. The last meeting of the R.D.C. before local government reform was held on 23 March 1974. The meeting and a lavish luncheon which followed went on from 10.30 am to 4.00 p.m. and the "West Wales Guardian" reported the proceedings under the banner headline "A Long Time A' Dying," which some people thought was rather irreverent!

The R.D.C. was not the only body to become top heavy with

officials. Far from it! I remember a thirties photograph of the County Offices staff which showed about forty to fifty people altogether. The Education Department, for instance, at that period comprised a Director of Education, an Assistant Director who was also County Librarian, a chief clerk, a finance officer, a typist, two senior clerks and a junior! The Haverfordwest County Court office was staffed almost entirely by one man, Mr. Gwilym Griffiths, under the direction of the registrar, Mr. H.J.E. Price, while the National Farmers' Union county office was run by the county secretary, Mr. W.E. Lees, and one shorthand typist, Miss Elsie Owen. At police headquarters at the Castle, where I was a regular caller in my quest for news, the main office staff comprised Inspector (later Superintendent) C.B. James and two sergeants, Richard Davies and Ben Williams (both of whom also became Superintendents). They worked under the general supervision of Deputy Chief Constable John Wheeler, the Chief Constable at that time, Mr. F.T.B. Summers, being more or less a figurehead. There were two beat Sergeants and about half a dozen constables in Haverfordwest, although all the surrounding districts had their "village bobbies". It was a good system and most people were sorry to see it change.

These are just a few examples of the small staffs which ran affairs in the County Town. It was the same elsewhere; Napoleon's nation of shopkeepers had not yet given way to the nation of officials.

Mention of the Police Force produces a flood of memories. Every policeman on the beat was known to the public as a personality in his own right and they were divided roughly into two categories - those who were tremendously zealous and unyielding in the execution of their duties and those who were "not bad old boys". Probably the keenest policeman in Pembrokeshire's history was P.C. (later Sergeant) Bodman who, like Javert in "Les Miserables", had a somewhat exaggerated sense of his duty. He was stationed at Haverfordwest and later at Pembroke Dock and his name became known all over the county; indeed, he is still talked about by older people. Some called him "P.C. Bodkin" and there were those who thought that it really was his name!

Another diligent officer in Haverfordwest at the time was Sergeant D.H. Lewis, known to all as "Krucheon," and among others who enjoyed much popularity (mainly because they were fairly easy going) were P.C.s Jim Thomas, Tudor Thomas, Tom Harris and Stanley Henton. P.C. Sambrook, a noted personality, was the Chief Constable's unofficial chauffeur, but neither he nor his boss knew that when their car was parked outside the Shire Hall at nights - a regular occurrence - it was frequently taken by a group of local young men, to go for a trip into the countryside! These dare-devils knew that the Chief was at the County Club and that he never left before a certain hour - by which time the car was safely returned to its parking space. They were never caught.

At a time when police policy was to give as little information as possible to the press, the two sergeants at Haverfordwest Police Station (Richard Davies and Ben Williams,) were usually helpful to me, provided the Inspector was not around. They were great practical jokers. Innocent visitors like myself would find themselves being frisked for "stolen property" or pushed into a cell and locked up for ten minutes. Once my bicycle disappeared and the two sergeants made great play of investigating "the crime". Then the machine mysteriously re-appeared! A more daring prank was to sprinkle water on Inspector James' chair and await results. I don't know whether the Inspector ever sat in it or whether he guessed what was happening, but it was his pet poodle which always had the blame! In those days all police prosecutions in the Magistrates' Courts were conducted by senior officers, usually Superintendents. By and large they did a difficult job with great competence as many a defending solicitor found out. The "star," undoubtedly, was C.B. James whose knowledge and quick wits, not to mention his supreme self-confidence, earned him great respect. His "court battles" with solicitors like Mr. William Evans of Fishguard and Mr. Bentley Mathias of Narberth, were real entertainment - 'better than the cinema' as they used to say. Once when the Haverfordwest solicitor, Mr. J.E.P. Morris, was applying at Haverfordwest Court for a summer extension for the seaside pubs, he said "Visitors to the seaside want something to drink that is worth drinking. They don't want to go home clogged with cocoa, poisoned by tea and distended by mineral water". Without hesitation, Supt. James replied "I would suggest, Your Worships, that neither do visitors want to go home queer with beer, frisky with whisky or merry with sherry". Corny stuff, perhaps. But it amused the packed "gallery" in the court and perhaps the magistrates as well.

But C.B. did not always get away with it. Strongly opposing the grant of a licence for the County Hospital nurses' annual ball at Haverfordwest Market Hall, he criticised the previous year's event, saying "it had degenerated into a Bacchanalian orgy of excess". When the magistrates returned after a brief retirement, the chairman, Alderman J.W. Hammond, who was never one to mince his words, said "The bench has no hesitation in granting the licence," and he went on to this effect: "It so happened that I too attended last year's ball and I know that the event was conducted with perfect decorum. There is no justification whatever for the remarks made by the police and we are most concerned that a senior police officer should be guilty of such wild exaggeration". Resilient though he was, C.B. took a long time to get over that one!

In the twenties and thirties paternity cases occupied much of the time of the courts. Certain solicitors, in the public view anyway, specialised in this type of case and the long reports in the local newspapers giving the most intimate details were read with avid interest. Regularly, the unmarried mother claimed that she had no doubt about the vital date because it was after the chapel anniversary, and the lawyers seldom failed to make great play of this. The poor girls involved usually had to go through hell in the witness box and, even then, often failed to get their 7/6d a week!

I remember the Press descending in force on a North Pembrokeshire rural court for the hearing of a paternity case. The special interest was that the girl alleged that her child was the result of what had occurred on the back seat of an Austin Seven motor car but the defendant, a tall man with broad shoulders, claimed that it was a physical impossibility. The whole case turned on this question. If my memory serves me the magistrates, in their wisdom, after viewing the car, found that the girl's story could be true - provided one of the doors was open!

Yes, they were colourful days and almost unbelievable by modern sophisticated standards. As Sam Goldwyn used to say, "a lot of water has passed since then!"

More and more as time went on, I found myself attending at the Shire Hall to report the courts (including the Assizes) and all sorts of County Council and other meetings. The hall became a sort of second home for nearly fifty years and while many may not have found that very attractive, to me it was a place of endless fascination - from the Press seats and, later, from the Bench.

CHAPTER FOUR

ON TOUR WITH GWILYM

"But what good came of it at last?"
quoth little Peterkin.
"Why, that I cannot tell" said he
"but 'twas a famous victory."
- *From the "Battle of Blenheim."*

After a great many years as Member of Parliament and Minister of the Crown, Gwilym Lloyd George was made a peer. He was "kicked up stairs" in the traditional way to make room for the younger man. It was said that when Macmillan asked him if he had decided on a title, Gwilym thought for a moment and then replied quietly "Well, there's a village in my old constituency of Pembrokeshire called Stepaside . . . . ". It was this sort of humour which helped to endear Gwilym Lloyd George to the Pembrokeshire people. It would hardly be an exaggeration to say that it helped more than his politics, which at all the elections I can remember were more than a little contrived. In the beginning he was a plain Liberal, then he was a "Lloyd George Liberal" (of course), then a "Liberal with Conservative support" and, in the end, a declared Conservative. That he continued to be successful for so long was a tribute to his personality. Gwilym was a master of the soft answer. He was the embodiment of what Pembrokeshire people call "a nice chap".

I "covered" Major Gwilym - as he was known to everyone - throughout the thirties and forties, reporting his speeches all over the constituency. Unlike his father, he was never a hell-raiser. But he had a good platform presence and the gift of being able to make the most unlikely arguments sound convincing. People liked him. He also leaned heavily on the Lloyd George name. His speeches always included references to "my father" and sometimes when he mentioned Megan as well, it became "our father" and he thus moved from the filial to the spiritual, which many people at the time thought appropriate having regard to the old man's God-like reputation.

Reporting the elections of the 1930's was something to remember. There were no press officers or hand-outs of speeches in those days;

reporters attended the meetings and reported the speeches as they were made, not only those of the candidate but those of the supporting speakers as well. It was a hard grind but great experience, and experience is a good thing as long as it doesn't kill you!

When Major Gwilym went on his nightly tours of the main towns and villages of the constituency, I was often in the entourage which accompanied him, it being the job of those in the party to go ahead of the candidate and "warm up" the audiences at the scheduled meeting places, pending the arrival of the great man. This often became hilarious. The candidate always got delayed because of questions etc. at the early meetings, with the result that before the night's programme was half-way through, he was about an hour behind schedule. Every meeting place - Freystrop, Hook, Llangwm, Rosemarket, Waterston and Neyland comprised a typical night's "tour" - would be packed with people and no matter how long the wait or late the hour they would stay put until the candidate arrived. There was much singing, shouting and stamping of feet.

Major Gwilym's supporting speakers, of course, had to "keep the pot boiling" until he arrived, a formidable task indeed. More than once, I saw supporting speakers dry up. The signs became familiar - the speaker would begin to repeat himself, then he would start speaking at a slower rate until literally there was a pause between each word and his desperation became apparent to all. Sometimes a speech would come to an abrupt full stop. The audience revelled in this and there would be cat-calls and derisory remarks although these were usually in good humour.

One supporting speaker whom I never saw dry up was Rev. J.B. Perkins, one of Gwilym Lloyd George's great henchmen who was Congregational minister at Milford Haven for many years and later lived at Keyston and then at Nolton. I usually travelled on these occasions in Rev. Perkins' car, in itself a memorable experience. A strong personality and gifted with a fiery eloquence, J.B. was more politician than minister of religion. He could whip up an audience into tremendous enthusiasm within minutes and was an expert in dealing with awkward questions. No one got the better of J.B! I liked him for several reasons. A terrible war wound had left him a cripple and in permanent pain yet he always contrived to be cheerful. For a Nonconformist pastor he was refreshingly broadminded. He was completely without humbug. If he felt like saying 'damn' or even worse, he said it - which in the thirties was something that was talked about. One of the first remarks I ever heard him make was "What's the matter with the bloody thing?" referring to a film projector which had broken down when he was giving a lecture at Keyston Chapel. The priests despite their shamming are not averse to gentle damning! I admired particularly his gift for the vivid phrase! As a young reporter, I was impressed at a peace meeting at the Palace Theatre, Haverfordwest - he was an ardent pacifist - to hear him declare "the glory of the sword is the rust thereof" (though I realised later this was probably a quotation.) And when the noted Welsh lawyer and Liberal leader Clement Davies K.C., severely criticised Pembrokeshire's record respecting the incidence of tuberculosis, J.B. dimissed it as "the injudicious remarks of an unjudicial K.C".

Much later, on a lighter note, I happened to be present when Mrs Perkins, after shopping, was trying unsuccessfully to open the door to the family car, assisted by prominent Haverfordwest businessman Mr.F.L. Green. After a few minutes, J.B. arrived and Mr.Green said rather crossly "We can't open the door". To which the reverend gentleman promptly replied "Well, you see, the doors of my car are like the gates of heaven - they don't open to every bloody fool who comes along".

Gwilym Lloyd George was well-known in Pembrokeshire long before he became the county's M.P. in 1922. Like other members of the family, he was a frequent visitor and during the 1914-18 war was stationed in Pembroke Dock for a time, enjoying much popularity among his fellow officers. On one occasion the police visited the Bush Hotel at midnight and found a small group of army officers enjoying a quiet drink in a back room, among them Gwilym Lloyd George, son of the Prime Minister. Not surprisingly the case never came to court!

After the war, Sir Evan Jones, Bart, one of the best public speakers the county has ever known, became Pembrokeshire's Liberal M.P. but in 1922 he gave way to Major Gwilym who was elected with a majority of nearly 12,000 in a straight fight with Labour's Mr.Willie Jenkins, farmer and former schoolteacher. The following year there was another General Election and Gwilym only just managed to hold on to the seat against the formidable opposition of Major (later Sir) Charles Price, Conservative. It was a troubled period in national politics and in 1924 the third election in three years was called and this time Sir Charles Price created a great sensation by wresting the seat from Major Gwilym with a majority of 1,500, the redoubtable Willie Jenkins coming third with 8,455 votes, a thousand less than he had "scored" the previous year. Unfortunately for

Major Price, Pembroke dockyard was closed soon afterwards and public opinion blamed him for it, probably without justification. The result was that he lost the seat in 1929, Major Gwilym being returned with a majority of 4,800, and he repeated the achievement in 1931 and 1935, this time against a new young Conservative champion, Mr. George Allison. By now, the Liberal majority had fallen to just over a thousand and after the war Gwilym could only muster a mere 168 majority against Labour's Major Wilfred Feinburgh, one of the new generation of young Socialists and a bonny fighter indeed. It was a clear indication of things to come . . . .

The 1945 Parliament ran its complete term and was full of controversy. Gwilym Lloyd George was prominent in national politics. However, he knew he was facing a tough fight at home, the Pembrokeshire Labour Party having adopted another young firebrand, Desmond Louis Donnelly who, although only 29, had already had the experience of fighting two Parliamentary campaigns. The 1950 election was held on a cold February day and in Pembrokeshire it was a straight fight between Donnelly and Lloyd George, now standing as a Liberal with Conservative support. Later, describing the count at the Market Hall, Haverfordwest, Desmond Donnelly wrote: "Knowing already that the total poll was 51,004, I watched the Lloyd George total mount towards 25,500, the magic halfway mark. It reached 25,250. At the last minute, I suddenly realised that it might not reach the next 250 . . . . . A hush settled in the hall. I nodded to Rosemary down the hall and saw her take in her breath. Slowly the enormity of what had happened dawned on the others present, quite five minutes after I had known. We were in by 141".

The Liberal agent, Mr. E.T. Thomas, demanded a re-count which lasted nearly two hours only to show that the Donnelly majority had increased to 152 but there were 23 votes missing. Desmond said he would give these to his opponent and Gwilym nodded silently. "He was very brave" said Donnelly. "We went outside (to declare the poll) and as I stepped out first behind Mr. Louis Underwood, the Returning Officer, there was a stunned silence. Then a yell went up. People cheered. People booed. One well-known Pembrokeshire farmer shook his fist at me in rage. Some Labour supporters were crying. The citadel had fallen, after 32 years".

It was the end of Gwilym's political association with Pembrokeshire. He joined the Conservative Party and secured the safe seat of Newcastle North where he served until created the first Viscount Tenby in 1957. He died in 1967 to the genuine regret of everyone in Pembrokeshire.

CHAPTER FIVE

THE GRAMMAR SCHOOL ROW

> A soft answer turneth away wrath;
> but grievous words stir up anger.
> - *Proverbs 15-1*

Two of the biggest public rows that I remember concerned the staff of the Grammar School at Haverfordwest and the salary of the Town Clerk at Pembroke. The Grammar School row erupted like a volcano from the ancient corridors in Dew Street, remained at fever pitch for many weeks and then died away so slowly that it was ten years before the "stigma" of having sacked five of its senior staff was finally and officially removed from the school. Mr.R.S. Lang was appointed headmaster of Haverfordwest Grammar School in January, 1927, at the age of 33. His ability was beyond dispute. He was all out to make a name for himself and the school, and improvements in discipline and academic results soon began to show. But after a few years he came to the conclusion that the really great things he had in mind for the school could never be realised without drastic changes.

At a Governors' meeting one day in 1933, the headmaster's report was adopted without much discussion even though it included a small item which recommended that the services of five assistant masters should be discontinued. The five were Mr.F.C.M. Richards, Mr. A. Mortimer, Mr. J. Aspinall, Mr. J. Burns and Mr. W.T. Francis. All were noted for their ability (in the public eye anyway) although it must be admitted that at least two had some eccentricity of behaviour. The boys in their way had a good deal of respect and affection for them. All the masters in those days had nicknames and those for the five concerned were "Bulgy" (Mr.Richards), "Morty" (Mr.Mortimer), "Aspy" (Mr.Aspinall), "Johnny" (Mr.Burns), and "Parley" (Mr.Francis) - not very imaginative except perhaps for "Parley Francis", and it must be said that "Bulgy" was typical of unintentional schoolboy cruelty as it arose from a facial disfigurement following a war wound which Mr.Richards had suffered. All the names were used freely (in the masters' absence of course!) and without the slightest malice. Incidentally, the headmaster at that time was always called 'Reggie' by the boys but in later years had the nickname 'Bull' for what reason I know not.

But if the Governors conveniently or through inadvertence paid little attention to the item about the masters, its significance did not escape the ever alert 'Guardian' reporter E. Lloyd Phillips. He recognised the recommendation for the dynamite it was, and there were big headlines in the "Guardian" that week and the dismissals became the talk of the town and district. In addition, a "Guardian" leading article written by the newspaper's owner and editor, Alderman J.W. Hammond, made an all-out attack on the headmaster and the Governors for their treatment of five old, publicly valued and greatly respected members of the staff.

The response to this publicity from people of all walks of life, and especially from old boys of the school, was extraordinary. Letters poured into the "Guardian" all deploring the action taken by the Governors. Old boys of the school holding responsible positions in various parts of the country, wrote to the editor to express disgust at what had happened. One letter I recall came from India. Articles appeared in educational journals, special meetings of teachers' bodies were held and many resolutions of protest were passed. Among other things it was pointed out that three of the masters were over fifty and the other two were over forty five and had no chance, "branded by dismissal," of securing other teaching posts.

Undoubtedly, public opinion was strongly in favour of the five masters but other voices were raised occasionally. For instance, the editor of the "Western Telegraph", Mr John Thomas, writing under his well-known nom-de-plume, "John Haverford," regretted that so much publicity had been given to the dismissals. "The unmeasured abuse heaped upon the Governors in certain quarters" he wrote "has needlessly embittered and stiffened the backs of the Governors and made it difficult, if not impossible, for them to yield . . . . . Well might the teachers pray to be delivered from their friends". John was a much admired commentator on local affairs but on this issue he found little support.

The campaign went on for weeks and the Governors held another meeting, but by nine votes to six they decided to adhere to their decision. This intransigence the "Guardian" described as something that had "literally horrified the whole educational establishment of this country". In bold type the newspaper continued - "Not only has the entire teaching profession been staggered by the idea that such a thing is possible but those in authority at Cardiff and Whitehall are deeply concerned and are earnestly considering what steps can be taken to deal with the unprecedented situation which has arisen. We use the word unprecedented advisedly because in the history of education in England and Wales for the last 27 years the action of the Governors is without parallel".

Then, on Alderman Hammond's suggestion, a public meeting was organised at the Masonic Hall early in 1934. The hall was packed to the doors and the atmosphere was electric as the leading protestors, including representatives of the Assistant Masters Association, the National Union of Teachers, various public authorities and of the clergy, took their places on the platform. Mr.W.S. Brewer, ex-serviceman and member of Haverfordwest Borough Council, presided and many hard-hitting speeches were made. I remember Mr.Harry Calderwood, a Milford Haven schoolmaster and chairman of the Wales Area of the British Legion, stressing the fact that the five masters were all ex-servicemen. Thumping the table, he declared "Not many years ago we used to sing 'It's a long way to Tipperary.' Now we should be singing 'It's a LANG way to Tipperary". This rather ridiculous remark drew thunderous applause. A resolution was passed describing the dismissals as indefensible and calling for the re-instatement of the masters. The resolution also asked the County Education committee to amend the scheme governing the Grammar School.

But when eventually the shouting and tumult began to die, the protesters had achieved very little. The headmaster and Governors agreed to reinstate one of the masters (Mr.Mortimer) for a year or so until he reached pensionable age. Another of the masters (Mr.Aspinall) was fortunate enough to secure a post at St. Davids County School but the other three had to go and were largely unemployed for the remainder of their lives. While it was a tragedy for these men it was an uneasy peace for the Grammar School and particularly for Mr.Lang. The Assistant Masters' Association "blacked" the school and for many years afterwards there was a standing advertisement in the Association journal warning its members against applying for posts at the school. The school was also "blacked" respecting sporting fixtures with other schools. It says much for Mr.Lang's strength of character, resourcefulness and ability that the school continued to be well-staffed and to achieve outstanding academic successes. In addition, Mr.Lang was eventually elected to the Headmasters' Conference and Haverfordwest Grammar School became a public school for the remainder of his headmastership.

Time is the great healer and it is interesting to record that it was Alderman Hammond, the leader of the campaign for the dismissed masters, who after the last war was mainly responsible for removing the black-listing of the school. By this time, Alderman Hammond was himself a Governor of the school and he was chairman of the Governors at the time of his death in 1954. He and the headmaster were now firm friends and the school paid Alderman Hammond a spectacular tribute at his funeral, the boys with heads bowed lining both sides of Dew Street as the cortege passed on its way to City Road Cemetery.

As a youth, not unnaturally, I regarded Mr.Lang as something of an ogre. But later, when I knew him well, I found him to be very human and, even more surprisingly, full of fun. During the years leading up to his retirement he used to send for me regularly and I always turned up, dutifully, at his study, only to find that all he wanted was to talk about some recent decision of the Education Committee or discover what people were saying about the latest Grammar School successes. Or, perhaps, he just wanted to gossip - I found him to be far more interested in the town and its personalities than I had believed. One day I raised the subject of the dismissed masters and ventured the suggestion that had he been less precipitate and spread the dismissals over a few years he might have saved himself a lot of trouble. But he wouldn't accept this. "My dear boy" he said "I couldn't wait that long. I had to act as I did in the interests of the school". I asked him if the row and its repercussions had affected his personal life very much. He agreed that it had but maintained that he had never been shaken in the conviction that his action was right in the interests of the school. Only half jokingly, he added: "As to my personal life, I'm sure I would have been a lot better off in Haverfordwest if only I had joined the Freemasons and attended Tabernacle Chapel!"

A few of Mr. J.W. Hammond's "Guardian Angels" photographed during a staff outing to Barry in June 1935.

Left to right : Back - Llewellyn Thomas (reporter), Jack Griffiths (compositor), Bill Richards (reporter).

Front : Lloyd Phillips (chief reporter), Bill Paton (sub-editor) and Harry Rogers (compositor).

Three members of the highly respected Owen family of Summerhill, near Keyston, who were such an influence for good in the locality. Reesy (centre) was a pioneer of the National Farmers' Union, a leading member of Haverfordwest Rural Council and one of the mainstays of Keyston Congregational Chapel, where for many years he was choirmaster and ran the Sunday School almost single-handed. With him here are two of his sisters, Ita (left) and Cissie.

Major Gwilym Lloyd George, Pembrokeshire's popular M.P., 1922 - 1924 and 1929 - 1950. He became Home Secretary and in 1957 was created the first Viscount Tenby of Bulford.

Mr. R.T. Griffiths and some of his senior scholars at the unique Camrose South School, circa 1927 - 1928.
Back: Cyril Evans, Tommy Willhams, Eddie John, Jim Evans, Vernon Thomas, Willie Watts.
Middle: Rose Owen, Mildred Wilcox, Sheila Roberts, Betty Griffiths, Mary Watts, Betty Roberts, Dilys Evans, Nesta Roberts, Flo Edwards.
Front: George Edwards, Ivor Rees, Willie Wilcox, Ronnie Evans, Albert Watts, Bill Richards.

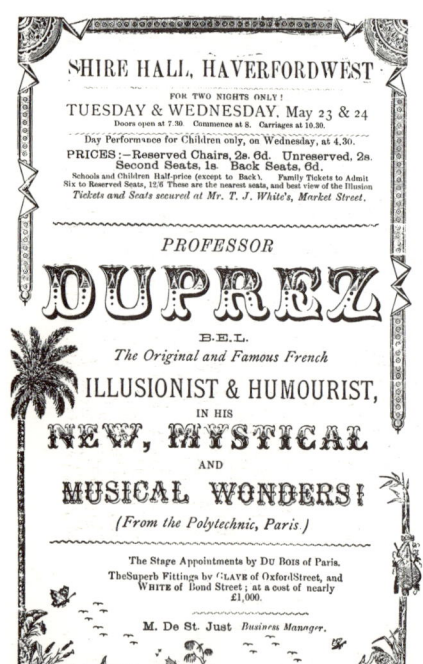

In the mid and late 1800's the Shire Hall was a popular centre of entertainment. All sorts of shows were staged there including that by the "famous Professor Duprez", who made several visits.

The Rev. J.B. Perkins' fiery oratory in the Liberal cause enlivened many a Pembrokeshire political meeting between the wars. In this photograph, taken about 1929 when he was Congregational minister in Milford Haven, he is seen (left) holding his daughter, Nest (now Mrs. Mathias, 61 Slade Lane, Haverfordwest), while Major Gwilym Lloyd George, for so long Pembrokeshire's M.P., is fourth from the left with his wife on his right. They were, of course, later to become Viscount and Lady Tenby. Others in the photograph include Mrs. Lloyd George's parents, Mr. E.T. Thomas, Dew Street, Haverfordwest (Liberal Agent), Mrs. J.B. Perkins and Miss Dora Lewis, Haverfordwest, a well known Liberal stalwart.

A reminder of the ceremonial of former days. Mr. Justice Hallett arrives at the Shire Hall, Haverfordwest, for the opening of the Summer Assizes in June, 1956, watched by a large gathering which thronged the nearby pavements. The judge is attended by the High Sheriff, Mr Norman Perkins, (back to camera) and his chaplain, Canon Richard Williams, Vicar of St. Martins.

This unique photograph was taken at the Haverfordwest celebration of the proclamation of King Edward VII in 1901. The huge crowd is standing alongside St. Mary's Church on what was formerly the site of Haverfordwest's old Guild Hall and where the South African war memorial was later erected.

Mr. G.W. John, noted headmaster of Camrose South School and valued member of Haverfordwest Rural District Council.

The Rev. David Garro Jones, one of the best known and most controversial Congregational ministers in South Wales during the earlier years of the century. He was pastor of Keyston and Nolton churches from 1924 to 1929 during which time his son, Capt. George Garro Jones, was Liberal M.P. for Hackney South and a prominent national figure. George became the first Lord Trefgarne.

The Rev. W.H. Williams, beloved pastor of Hill Park Baptist Church, devoted hospital worker and a loyal friend to the author during his early news gathering days. Mrs. Williams (left), a quiet, unassuming lady, provided the welcome cup of tea.

The outspoken William Roberts of East Dunston, Camrose South, who, unsuccessfully urging a "no smoking" rule at meetings of Haverfordwest Rural Council, told his colleagues "If God intended us to smoke he would have put a chimney in our heads". It took nearly fifty years for the wisdom of his remarks to be generally accepted!

The scourge of Haverfordwest R.D.C. officials during the war years, John Young, farmer, of St. Brides. Mr. Young, a proud Scotsman, came to Pembrokeshire as agent to the Kensington estate and became a successful farmer and prominent rural councillor. In retirement he lived at Haven Road, Haverfordwest

The Rev. E. Nicholson Jones (Tabernacle), a provider of piquant paragraphs.

William Hancock, Camrose farmer and prominent County and Rural District Councillor. He was the first Chairman of Pembrokeshire War Agricultural Executive Committee after the outbreak of hostilities in 1939.

Mr. H.J. Dickman, a well-known son of Llangwm, who succeeded Mr. W.D. Hill as Clerk and Chief Financial Officer to Haverfordwest Rural District Council and continued in the office with conspicuous ability until the Council disappeared under local government re-organisation.

The Shire Hall, a jewel in the Haverfordwest crown. For many generations vital matters concerning law and order, local government and the social life of the town and county have been conducted within this fine old building.   Photo: Norman Owen

Its structure, layout and decoration make the main hall of the Shire Hall a most impressive place and it is regarded as one of the best Court houses in the country. Some of its unique features are seen in this photograph taken when Mr. Donald Twigg was made Mayor of Haverfordwest in 1984. Seated in the big chair, usually reserved for the judiciary, is the outgoing Mayor, Mr. Brian Hearne.   Photo: Norman Owen

As indicated in the early chapters of this book, music and singing played a big part in the social life of Haverfordwest and district in former days, although the Haverfordwest Choral Society (above) had disappeared by the 1930's. Included in this remarkable photograph, circa 1912, are some extremely well known local people: W.E. Dixon (conductor). Col. Jones (lawyer), Frank Mullins (professional singer), F. Langford (stationmaster), Percy Wilkins (ironmonger) and Mrs. Wilkins, Rupert Davies, Mrs. Rupert Davies, (later Mrs. Thomas, Dew Street), Nurse Baggott,, Miss Winnie Sinnett, Miss M. Michael, Miss Barber, J. and J.P. Reynolds (grocers), Louie Phillips (Mill House), Gladys Dixon, Lily Adams, (Wellington Inn, Prendergast), Mrs. E. Clarke, Mrs. D. Morgan, Don Roberts, Des Roberts, Mrs. M Braithwaite, William Evans (Flannel Shop), Jack Phillips (Bland's), Sammy Rogers, George Phillips (Dew Street), Isaac Edwards, Jim James, David Lewis and Mrs. Lewis (Prendergast Place), Mrs Mary Ann Hammond, Miss Ethel Mckenzie, Misses Davies, (Prendergast House), James Sinnett, Dolly Phillips, Agnes Harrison, Mary Phillips, Jimmy Price, Martha Price, Owen Dixon, W. Allen, Insurance agent (North Street), Austin Davies (Prendergast), Lottie Morgan (Prendergast), Tommy Price (Barn Street), Maybro Phillips (Bridge Street), Louis Reynolds, Mrs. Birch, Tilly Jenkins, Mr. Leighman (Bridge Street.), George Pettit (North Street), Cora Morgan, Louise Reynolds, Lettie Edwards (later Mrs.Sidney Rees), Mrs. Seth Griffiths, Mrs. Walton.

CHAPTER SIX

PROSPERITY COMES TO THE COUNTRYSIDE

> Government of the people,
> by the people and for the people
> shall not perish from the earth.
> - *Abraham Lincoln*

One of the great changes wrought by the last war was the prosperity it brought to the rural areas. In the twenties and thirties all rural development was inhibited by grinding poverty. The few regarded as being well off, mostly the so-called "big farmers", were not really prosperous; they just owned more than the majority, many of whom were literally on the breadline. With the war, when national survival became more important than money, the whole picture changed. So that Britain should not starve, the Government poured cash into food production through subsidies, grants and other measures, and in the Pembrokeshire countryside, as elsewhere, things began to look up. In the early years of the war I attended many farm and other demonstrations in various parts of the county and was amazed to see all the new machinery in use and the sophisticated methods now employed, all for the war effort. Money was no object. As a layman, I wondered why it had taken a war to create such prosperity.

The good times, money-wise, went on for many years and fortunes were amassed, even on the smallest farms. Not that the farmers ever admitted it! Every annual meeting of the National Farmers' Union at Haverfordwest was crisis time if one believed the farmers, who attended in their hundreds and by now had developed an extraordinary volubility! There was always an emergency of some sort. The local newspapers looked forward to the early potato season because the farmers' "big losses" each year were certain to produce correspondingly big headlines. Outside of agriculture, all this was taken philosphically and most people managed a wry smile as the farmers came into town - as they did most days - in their big Rovers. I went for the truth to my old friend, Willie John, who farmed on a moderate scale at Lambston, near Haverfordwest. "Look here, boy" he would say in his pronounced Pembrokeshire accent "we farmers have been doing well for years now. If there's a farmer about who can't make a bit of money these days, well, there's something wrong with'n". Willie John was the only farmer who ever frankly admitted to me that he was prospering. It should be made clear, of course, that the new-found wealth on the land also benefited the towns. In a predominantly agricultural area, the farmer's prosperity meant everybody's prosperity and this applied especially to Haverfordwest which was the main shopping centre of the old county of Pembroke.

Concomitant with the changes in the countryside were the huge developments undertaken by Haverfordwest Rural District Council. With money to handle, the country folk wanted a higher standard of living, and the RDC gave it to them - in the form of modern houses, water and sewerage schemes, improvement grants, public lighting and so on. There was no stint. In the little village of Keyston, the Council provided more street lamps than there were houses, which was criticised at the time but it must be said that since then the village has grown considerably, so perhaps it was not so extravagant after all. I am not claiming that Haverfordwest RDC was the only local authority in Pembrokeshire to contribute to the rural revolution. Far from it. But having had a long and close association with that Council, I know something of the work it did, especially in the villages in the area, all of which have improved beyond recognition when compared with pre-war years. Its record is worth a little space. The re-organisation of Haverfordwest Rural Council which led to it becoming one of the leading local authorities in the country started in 1942, and as it happened to coincide with my return to Haverfordwest to work I was able to watch its progress at first hand. The first meetings I attended at this stage, now held at the Shire Hall and so different from the workhouse meetings of ten years before (mentioned in an earlier chapter) were dominated by a gentleman of rare single-mindedness - John Young, a well-known St. Brides farmer. Mr.Young, a Scot who, incidentally, was a director of St. Mirren Football Club, would rise and in the pronounced accents of his homeland, put question after question to the Clerk, Mr.Walter V. Evans. He was after the Clerk's blood and he never let up. At this distance in time I can't remember the details but the upshot of it all was that the Council appointed a Financial Officer, William Dodd Hill, and in the following year the Clerk resigned. Mr. Hill then became Clerk and Chief Financial Officer. About this time, the Council also appointed a number of other officals, including Mr. A.J. Davies, later Chief Planning Officer to Preseli Council, all of whom were bubbling with ideas about expansion.

William Dodd Hill was an unobtrusive man but he had great ability and, perhaps even more important, he had friends at the Welsh Office, which ensured that he had the best guidance possible in all the big projects which the Council was to undertake. I remember an occasion when Mr. Hill hit the headlines by refusing to take a pay increase. The item appeared in the "Daily Mail" in black type under the heading "Money Is The Root . . . . . Take Away, Take Away, Take It Away". The RDC was fortunate, also, in having many prudent and far-sighted members - men like Rees Owen (Roch), William Hancock (Camrose), T.P. Cousins (Freystrop), James John (Llangwm), Jim Philpin (Broad Haven), whose sharp wit and outspokenness enlivened many a meeting, Paxton Davies (Milford Haven), T.H.H. Walters (Trancredston), the brothers Perry and Idris Martin (St. Davids), and many others. These were the men who, with the officials' backing, pushed the schemes forward. They were later joined by a younger generation of councillors, prominent among whom for several years were G.W. John (Camrose) and Jack Sheppard (Haverfordwest). These two, known to some as the "terrible twins" helped tremendously in keeping the Council on its toes - Mr. John with logical, usually unanswerable arguments aways lucidly expressed, and the abrasive Mr. Sheppard jumping in where angels feared to tread with questions and speeches on all aspects of Council work. It was rapier and broadsword, and between them the two made a great contribution to the Council's effectivness. Another councillor of sound common sense was Walter Thorne, the Studdolph farmer and noted cattle breeder. He led the opposition to the establishment of the county of Dyfed, which he forecast would be "an officials' paradise" (how right he was!), opposed "Preseli" as the name for the new District Council and, practically single-handed, started the campaign which led to the abandonment of a proposed refuse pulverisation scheme near the Bolton Hill reservoir.

Haverfordwest RDC always had more than its fair share of "characters". One who, I'm sure, was much misunderstood was Kenneth Walker, the monocled squire of Boulston. He hardly ever smiled but, in fact, had a highly developed sense of humour. He was interested in all local affairs and contributed regularly to the "Guardian" correspondence columns, his letters being addressed either to "The Printer's Devil, Market Street, Haverfordwest" or to "The * Reporter" (The Star Reporter). Sometimes his letters came from Monte Carlo where he was wont to go on holiday. Once when Mr. John Gwyther of Pembroke wrote to the "Guardian" that he was staggered by some proposed expenditure, Mr. Walker replied the following week with a letter which commenced "In answer to staggered Mr. Gwyther ...." At the RDC meetings, Kenneth Walker made great play of his objection to opening the proceedings with prayer. "This is hypocrisy - the Lord isn't interested in Haverfordwest RDC" he would declare before ostentatiously leaving the room. When the prayer was over he would return noisily and resume his seat looking extremely fierce, but those who knew him well realised that the whole thing was just a leg-pull. He certainly annoyed some members by his "irreverent" attitude but this, of course was the object of the exercise! Two ministers of religion, the Rev. G. Nicholas of Wolfcastle and Rev. Howell Phillips, Tiers Cross, both useful members of the Council, were particularly put out by the squire's behaviour!

A member who annoyed the others in a different sort of way was Sidney Mortimer of St. Davids. He was a sea-faring man and inordinately proud of the fact. He didn't know the meaning of the word modesty. Regularly questions concerning the coast, the sea or the tides arose during Council discussions and this was always the signal for Sidney Mortimer to be on his feet. "I don't know why the officals didn't consult me on this" he used to say. "I'm a seafaring man and I know all about this. I know it like the back of my hand". Members seeking his vote would sometimes refer to him as "Captain Mortimer". He loved the title, but his vote was not so easily bought. He held strong views and usually stuck to them through thick and thin. In many ways he was a good councillor; he was completely fearless and worked with exceptional zeal on behalf of St. Davids. He was a real live wire. But his value to St. Davids and the Council would have been enhanced had he been less quarrelsome. When Herbert Morse (Scleddau), a quiet, intelligent member was chairman of the Council, he ruled S.W. Mortimer out of order over some unimportant matter. It was the signal for a vitriolic attack by the St. Davids member. He called the chairman "an idle layabout who was living on the State", etc. etc. - just because Mr.Morse was in extremely poor health at the time and was unable to work. It was a totally unwarranted attack for which he was never forgiven by some members.

Of an entirely different type was Willie John of Lambston, to whom I have already referred. He was bluff and genial, a real countryman who never spoke in anger. He was loved by the Council for his transparent honesty. He could also be extremely funny, often unwittingly. When the County Planning Officer, Mr. Jack Price, objected to what was said to be a new opening on to the highway at Keyston Hill, Mr. John protested at RDC meetings, claiming that it was not a new opening at all. "I drove hay through an opening there when I was a boy" he declared, adding after a pause "I don't suppose Price the Planning ever drove hay through there." Objecting to some proposed expenditure, Mr. John exclaimed: "When I read about this it made my hair stand on end" - and the meeting roared because he was completely bald. In his book on the RDC Mr. H.J. Dickman (a former Clerk to the Authority) relates how Willie John pooh-poohed the idea of the Council employing a Rodent Officer with the comment: "All we want is a couple of good cats", and when the Council congratulated his sons on coming first and second in the Welsh clay shooting championships he said "I don't know what was the matter with those boys - they only got 98 per cent".

It is possible to refer to only a few of the personalities who made up this purposeful Council. But I would like to mention Caleb Watts, the able and popular member for Spittal. After years of service, he was appointed vice-chairman in 1973 but he knew full well that he would not reach the chair because it was the last year of the Council's life before amalgamation. In typically witty manner Caleb commented: "I am like Moses. I view the Promised Land but I will never reach it". Despite his undoubted ability, Caleb was never one to be unduly ambitious and he accepted the loss of the chairmanship philosophically. His wit enlivened many a dull meeting. Once when making a speech he was interrupted repeatedly on "a point of order" by Canon Richard Williams, the vicar of St. Martins and a particularly talkative member. Caleb paused, looked at the chairman and asked "Will no one rid me of this turbulent priest?" It brought the house down and Canon Williams, who was a good sport, joined heartily in the laughter.

It must not be assumed that the RDC was always free of criticism. There were always complaints - about schemes, about priorities, house lettings, extravagance, overstaffing, the Council's attitude to various public questions, and so on. I remember a big row when the Council let a dwelling to an Italian farm worker - at a time when local families could not find decent accommodation for love or money. But overall the RDC did a good job, contributing immensely to the new prosperity and standards of life in the countryside.

CHAPTER SEVEN

WINNERS AND LOSERS

> Well, no offence, There ain't no sense
> In getting riled
> - *Bret Harte*

Before the box took over and began saturating our lives with sex and violence and interminable verbiage, people had a real interest in general and local government elections. Forty years ago a famous speaker like, say, Nye Bevan, could pack the Market Hall at Haverfordwest to the doors, and twenty years before that at least a thousand people would turn out just to hear the results of the Municipal elections in the Pembrokeshire Boroughs. In those days the Municipal elections were held in November when the weather was usually at its worst, but this did not stop people from going out to vote and, late the same night, facing the elements again in order to hear how the candidates had fared. People took the Council seriously and being a councillor placed a man on a pedestal, no matter what his limitations or personal character. Today, membership of a local authority is inclined to be regarded with cynicism by the general public. A councillor is no longer a big shot, although the man himself (or woman) might disagree.

In the old days the count at Haverfordwest was held at the Corn Market in Hill Street and the poll was declared from an upstairs window to a sea of faces and, usually, umbrellas below. A regular candidate was Mr. William McKenzie, the Victoria Place businessman, who had served on the Council for a few terms but somehow lost public confidence and year after year found himself among the "non-elected". He used to come to the window to thank his supporters and start by shouting "Still Outside". This became a sort of slogan and the crowd always waited for McKenzie's "Still Outside", and roared when it came. Amusements were simple in those days. There were four places to be filled on the Haverfordwest Borough Council each year and there were usually six or seven candidates. But the war put an end temporarily to elections and Councils remained unchanged from 1938 to 1945, except vacancies which were filled by co-option. The result of such a long period without elections was an extraordinary contest in Haverfordwest in November 1945, when there were no fewer than fifteen candidates for eight seats. It created tremendous interest, not only because of the long interregnum but also because, with the war over, a great resurgence of politics was taking place throughout the country and the Labour Party, having just won the general election hands down, were now putting candidates in the field everywhere. In Haverfordwest in November 1945, there were four official Labour candidates. It was the first time ever that Party labels had been adopted openly in a Haverfordwest election and the result was eagerly awaited. Alas for the Labour Party, they were in for a big disappointment, not one of their men finding a place. Haverfordwest showed for the first time, but not the last, that it is not a very politically-motivated town.

I did not cover that 1945 election in Haverfordwest, having gone to London to be entertained to dinner at The Dorchester by Lord Beaverbrook (a memorable occasion, but that's another story) and I got the result during a stop-off at Reading on the way home. It gave me great personal pleasure because my old boss, Alderman J.W. Hammond, editor and managing director of the "Guardian", topped the poll out of the fifteen, a fine achievement and a fitting reward for his valued service to the town over so many years.

The full result was as follows:-

ELECTED

J. W. Hammond	1839
Ralph Warren	1829
Claude Davies	1734
Eddie Jones	1687
R.F. Foster	1632
Ivor Lloyd	1542
Leslie H. Ellis	1443
Ivor Male	1428

NOT ELECTED

L.T. Fisher (Lab)	1353
T.D. Evans (Lab)	1302

George Twigg (Lab)	1217
Jack Edwards (Lab)	975
George Williams	764
D.J. Evans	717
W.E. Westfield	213

The Labour Party took their defeat badly. The local leaders seemed to think that following the landslide in the country, election to the local authorities would follow as a matter of course. One aspect which, apparently, was never fully appreciated was that the leaders in the local Party were in the main not "Harfats" but men from industrial areas who had moved to Haverfordwest to live - men like Jack Edwards (insurance company manager) and T.D. Evans (schoolmaster) who, while they provided the dynamism, were unable to understand the fundamental political difference between South Wales and Pembrokeshire.

L.T. Fisher lost a by-election later in 1945 but he topped the poll in November 1946. T.D. Evans, however, was not so successful. He was among the "not elected" in 1946 while in February 1947, he lost again at a by-election, securing 707 votes against Rowland Jones' 886. This third defeat in just over a year was too much for Trevor Evans. In his speech after the declaration of the poll he lashed out at the Tories, the pubs, the clubs, and even the Press, all of whom he claimed had combined to keep him out. It was the first time in Haverfordwest's history that a defeated candidate had lost his temper and it did Mr. Evans, and the Labour Party a lot of harm. Wisely, he kept out of the election picture for a few years. It was 1951 before he stood again, once more unsuccessfully, but in 1953 he secured election, the bad manners of 1947 finally forgotten, and in 1956 gained a great personal triumph by topping the poll. One of the other defeated Labour candidates of 1945, George Twigg also became a councillor eventually, and a useful one, but the fourth, Jack Edwards, never made it which was a great pity as he was an exceptionally able man whose work for his Party as speaker, writer and organiser was invaluable. His presence at Town Council meetings would have livened things up no end!

Intensive canvassing - going from door to door asking people for their votes - used to be regarded as an essential part of any election campaign. But then a new type of candidate began to emerge - the type who said "I am offering myself for the Council. If the people want me they can vote for me. If not, it doesn't matter". So canvassing today is on a much reduced scale. I am convinced, however, that there is no better way to ensure success at the polls than to go knocking on the doors. A really keen candidate should be prepared to take a week off, at least, to do this. The people like to be asked for their vote and appreciate the effort put in by the man prepared to make the rounds and discuss matters with them. I remember the experience of Ivor Male, a member of Haverfordwest Borough Council for many years. He was up for re-election in 1947 but was generally regarded as not having much of a chance, due probably to some stand he had taken in the Council Chamber. A few days before the election a friend warned him "Ivor, I'm afraid you're going to be out". Straightaway, Ivor got down to canvassing in earnest and for nearly a week, from early morning to late at night, he tramped the streets of the town. He reckoned he visited every house. He also did the rounds in a car equipped with a loud speaker and caused much amusement by announcing in stentorian tones "This is Ivor Male speaking to you in his own voice". And when the time came he topped the poll, a hundred votes ahead of the field!

It is extremely rare for a tie to occur in any election but this happened in at least two Haverfordwest Rural District Council contests. Just after the war, Mr. Stanley James and Mr. Jim Codd got an equal number of votes in Marloes, and the Presiding Officer, Mr. Leonard Warlow, a most able and courteous member of the RDC staff, had the unenviable task of giving a casting vote, which was the legal way of settling such an issue at the time. He gave his vote for Mr. James, no doubt influenced by the fact that Mr. James was the retiring member and had also for many years been chairman of the RDC's important Water Committee. Afterwards, there was talk of a High Court petition over the matter but Mr. Warlow had acted in a perfectly proper manner and eventually it all fell through. Several years later there was a similar occurrence at Merlins Bridge where the two candidates getting equal votes were Mr. Edwin Jenkins, Bethany, (the sitting member) and Mr. Bertie Davies, Dredgeman Hill. After the votes had been counted, and re-counted, and the tie was established beyond doubt, Mr. Davies sportingly said he would withdraw so that Mr. Jenkins could continue on the Council, on which he had served for so long. But it was found that this gesture, though generous, was illegal. The law had by now been changed and the candidates were required to draw lots - and when this was done Mr. Davies "won", and he went on to become a most useful member of the Council.

Another unusual occurrence followed a County Council election in Haverfordwest in the 1960's. The successful candidates, Mr. C.B. James (a former Deputy Chief Constable of Pembrokeshire) had a sizeable majority over his opponent, fellow Borough councillor Mr. D.J. Evans, but after the election a formal complaint was made that Mr. James had committed an offence. It transpired that during the campaign Mr. James had circulated an election message - a postcard if I remember - from which the printer's imprint at the bottom "Printed by . . . . . and Published by the Candidate" had been omitted. Most people would regard this as a triviality but it was a breach of election law and, a complaint having been made, action had to be taken. The result was that Mr. James and the printer, Mr. Gwyn Rowlands (Criterion Press, Bridge Street) were served with summonses and the case was heard at a special sitting of Haverfordwest magistrates. A solicitor came from London to prosecute. Mr. James conducted his own defence with the expertise of one who had spent a great part of his working life in the Courts. He admitted the offence but poured scorn on the whole thing. It was, he said, a classic case of the sledgehammer and the nut. Mr. D.J. Evans sat listening in the public gallery as Mr. James said witheringly "Apparently, someone laid this complaint against me hoping that by so doing he would be given the seat which I won". The magistrates agreed with Mr. James. They gave him and Mr. Rowlands (who wrote pleading guilty to an oversight) a conditional discharge.

The case was the talk of the town for a week or so. Most people thought it a waste of time and public money, especially as the offence did not invalidate the election and Mr. James retained his seat. It would have been a gross travesty had it been otherwise. Many questions were asked about how the proceedings came to be instituted, most people taking the view that a caution would have been an appropriate way of dealing with the matter. Mr. Evans made no secret of his part in the affair. But many suspected that he had been persuaded to take the ill-considered action by someone else who had kept well behind the scenes. In any event the matter occasioned bitter enmity, so much so that Mr. Evans and Mr.James never ever spoke to each other again.

CHAPTER EIGHT

TURBULENT YEARS

> My candle burns at both ends;
> It will not last the night:
> But ah my foes and oh my friends
> it gives a glorious light.
> - *Edna St. Vincent Millay*

In the nineteen twenties one of the great political "hopes" at Westminister was a Pembrokeshire man, Captain George Garro Jones, son of the Rev. David Garro Jones, Congregational minister. Captain Garro, as he was known, was born at Spittal manse, became Liberal M.P. for Hackney South in 1924 (defeating the prominent Labour leader Herbert Morrison) and, within a year, had made a name for himself in the House of Commons. It was said that he "could not possibly go further than he had planned". History more or less repeated itself thirty years later when Pembrokeshire's first Labour M.P., Desmond Louis Donnelly, had gained national prominence and was being widely tipped as a future leader. The comments about Garro Jones applied precisely to Desmond Donnelly. Desmond entered the House of Commons determined that England should hear him. He was also outrageously ambitious. Garro Jones was first a Liberal and then a Socialist for many years and became a Socialist peer (Lord Trefgarne) before returning to be a Liberal again. Donnelly covered an even wider political spectrum, moving from Common Wealth to Left Wing Socialist to Right Wing Socialist to Democrat to Conservative. He was a man of tremendous potential who brought a new dimension to the political life of Pembrokeshire. Who could have foreseen when he was at the height of his power and popularity in Pembrokeshire that such an outstanding career would end with a handful of pills and a bottle of vodka in a lonely London hotel bedroom?

When Desmond Donnelly first came to Pembrokeshire not long before the 1950 election he was a slim 29-year-old, recently married and diffident in manner almost to the point of shyness. He had strong Labour Party backing. After he had beaten Gwilym Lloyd George in the 1950 election - by 129 votes - there was a rapid change in the Donnelly personality and soon he was to be seen striding along the streets of

Pembrokeshire with tremendous self-assurance. In his first year as M.P. he made a great impact. In the constituency he was incredibly active; in Westminister he was referred to as "the brilliant new Member for Pembroke". When his 129 majority in the 1950 straight fight jumped to a staggering 9,026 majority in the three-cornered contest in 1951, the character change was complete and from then on Desmond Donnelly dominated the Pembrokeshire political scene.

It was soon evident that he had set his sights on the summit, that he "could not go further than he had planned". He was the real political animal. His ability was beyond doubt, he had unbounded enthusiasm and a prodigious capacity for hard work. But there were other sides to his mercurial character. He had about him a recklessness which worried his friends. I remember Trevor Evans, the Haverfordwest Labour stalwart, describing how Desmond used to drive his little car at break-neck speeds when returning from political meetings late at night, so that some refused to travel with him. One night, according to Trevor, he drove down Arnold's Hill at full throttle all the way, his three passengers - all heavyweight men - begging him to ease up while Desmond roared with laughter and kept shouting "I'll scare the daylights out of you bastards". I think Trevor Evans was one of the first to discern the Donnelly character weaknesses. More than once he talked to me in somewhat critical terms of his close association with Donnelly, and would add meaningfully "No man is a hero to his valet".

Desmond also developed an arrogance which made him impatient of the advice of more cautious friends. Many times I advised him that some action or other which he was proposing would do him no good, to which the reply was always the same - "I'm not concerned about doing myself good. If they kick me out of Pembrokeshire I can always go to the South of France and write novels". The writing novels bit was a pipe dream; the only novel he wrote made no impact. He reached a stage eventually when he paid no attention at all to advice - he literally didn't listen - and everyone who disagreed with him became "a bloody fool". The first indication that Pembrokeshire had of its M.P's unpredictability came at a Labour Party Conference at Scarborough in the early fifties when, out of the blue and in a dramatic fashion calculated to gain the maximum publicity, Donnelly rounded on his close friend, Nye Bevan, over the re-armament issue. It amazed everyone and greatly dismayed his friends. This was Donnelly's first major change as an M.P; he was no longer a left winger. It was said at the time that he had been paid £1,000 by the influential American "Time" magazine to make the attack on Nye, but Desmond swore to me that this was untrue. After the Conference, Nye and Desmond met face to face unexpectedly in a bar where a large number of Labour Party leaders were relaxing. It was a dramatic moment. "Let me buy you a drink", said Desmond, as if nothing had happened between them, to which Nye, a master of the quick retort, replied, "What will you use to pay for it - the thirty pieces of silver?" and turned on his heel.

After leaving the Left Wing, Desmond became a close associate of Hugh Gaitskell, who succeeded Attlee as Leader of the Labour Party in 1955. This, I think, was a happy period in Desmond's career. There was a mutual admiration between the two and Gaiskell's untimely death was not only a great personal loss to Donnelly but a blow to his political aspirations. Donnelly always claimed that but for Gaitskell's death he would have gone on to hold high office, in the Foreign Office, the Ministry of Education or the Ministry of Transport. I can quite believe that Gaitskell might have given him his chance. And that he could have been a brilliant success - or a calamity!

Donnelly went on actively to support George Brown for the Party leadership. Undoubtedly, he had his reasons for this, but it turned out to be a great mistake as far as his career was concerned. "He is backing the wrong horse again", people were saying in Pembrokeshire, and so it turned out. Wilson won and Donnelly's chances of office disappeared. When Labour came to power, he told me "Wilson offered me an obscure job, you know, a sort of Lord High Executioner for Scotland, but I wasn't having that". This was the beginning of the long-running feud between them that led to Donnelly's downfall.

During his twenty years in Pembrokeshire Desmond Donnelly was known nowhere better than at the "West Wales Guardian" offices in Haverfordwest, except perhaps at Labour Party headquarters. He had an acute awareness of the value of the Press to the politician, having made a close study of the expertise of Lloyd George in this field, and a week never passed in which he failed to call at or telephone the "Guardian" office, sometimes on several occasions. He was always alert and bubbling with ideas. He was also entertainingly frank about behind-the-scenes political moves and about politicians' private affairs. Through its close contact with him the "Guardian" was probably one of the best-informed weekly newspapers in the country on political affairs. He also wrote a weekly article for the "Guardian" which continued over the whole of his period in

Pembrokeshire. It was widely read and regarded as one of the newspaper's most valuable features. More than one offer was made to tempt Donnelly away from the "Guardian" but, while he was being accused of disloyalty on all sides in other respects, he refused steadfastly to write for any other local newspapers. He told me "The 'Guardian' gave the Labour Party and me publicity in the early days when nobody else wanted to know us. We could never have been successful without that and I will not forget it". He did not, but others did.

In the early years he used to give cocktail parties for close supporters at his new home at Roch. These were delightful affairs. As the punch flowed, animated conversation moved from politics to all sorts of topics, and Desmond was regarded by all as a splendid fellow. The horizons were clear: there was no sign or suggestion of aggro. A little later we were surprised to learn that he was also entertaining other people, like leading Conservatives and Pembrokeshire landowners. His friends didn't like it; it wasn't generally appreciated that Desmond was trying to establish himself on a wide base. In fact, in his hey-day in Pembrokeshire he commanded immense support from all Parties. He set an unrivalled example as a constituency Member. During the whole of his time as an M.P. he spent each week in London and each weekend in Pembrokeshire, returning on the sleeper every Sunday night.

He continued this grinding routine with cheerful resolution and on special occasions would visit the constituency in mid-week as well, often flying to Withybush to save time. He was always controversial. He was brilliant, rumbustious, unpredictable - a barnstormer with more than a fair share of charm. His generosity could be embarrassing. Because he was a chameleon in politics and had a rough tongue, he made many enemies. But throughout the twenty turbulent years, his greatest enemy was himself.

During his much publicised attacks on Labour policies and his bitter feud with Harold Wilson from the mid-sixties on, Desmond told me several times that he would never leave the Party. "You cannot succeed that way," he would say, referring to what had happened to Sir Oswald Mosley, and quoting Churchill's advice to the ambitious - "Make sure of your base". This was one of the reasons why he looked after his constituency so assiduously. How, then, did it come about that a man of such outstanding ability and devotion should have fallen by the wayside? There is no doubt that his burning ambition, his impatience and his scorn of traditional time-serving contributed to his downfall, but it was his attitude towards the Labour leader which brought it all to a head. From 1964 on, the enmity grew and grew until it became obsessional, on Donnelly's side anyway, and although he still had a huge following, his reputation began to suffer. In retrospect, the absurdity of the position is clear; how could a lone back-bencher M.P., even one with Donnelly's talents, hope to take on a Party leader like Wilson and hope to win? For years, Donnelly maintained a relentless, vicious campaign, and in all that time Wilson never deigned to answer him. To all appearances, as far as Wilson was concerned, Donnelly did not exist. It was a case of David and Goliath - with Goliath winning hands down. It was inevitable that eventually he would be expelled from the Labour Party. When it happened, he still hoped for the support of the Pembrokeshire Constituency Party. But there had been ominous rumblings within the local Party for some time; several of its leaders were wondering how much longer they could continue with their maverick M.P.

The crunch came at a tumultuous, bitter, never-to-be-forgotten meeting at Willie Jenkins' House, in Dew Street, Haverfordwest, on April 6th, 1968, when the Pembrokeshire Party finally decided that it would have to do without Desmond Louis Donnelly. After all the hard work, all the care, all the devotion, he had lost "his base". But even then Desmond carried on in the same reckless way, driven by a force compounded of hope, resilience and unabating ambition. In the weeks leading up to the April 6th meeting it was obvious that it was going to be important. It was expected that it might become rowdy. It turned out to be sensational! There was a full turn-out of members, who hurried into the building, making no comment to the dozen or more journalists standing outside. The Press knew that the meeting was to be held in private but they turned up just the same, characteristically hopeful of getting a good story in some way or other. For once the optimism was justified. Although the meeting was held behind closed doors in the upstairs room, someone had rather thoughtlessly opened all the windows - it was a very hot day - and the reporters just stood together underneath and listened incredulously to the rip-roaring row which went on inside for nearly half-an-hour!

At the time of the meeting Desmond had already been expelled by the Labour Party and, strictly, had no right to attend. The reporters wondered whether the people at the door, who had sternly turned back the Press, would have the nerve to try and stop the M.P. from entering the building. There was no chance! Desmond, always an expert in public relations, left his car not outside Willie Jenkins' House but somewhere down on the Pig Bank and then walked up Dew Street in a sort of one-man triumphal procession, shaking hands with passers-by, waving and shouting cheery greetings. At the door of Willie Jenkins' House he stopped to have a few words with the reporters, shaking hands and using first names all round, and then he bounded up the steep stairs, ignoring the doorkeepers, and took a place at the top table. The row that developed inside was unbelievable. It became so disorderly that, from underneath the window by the Catholic Church, a lot of it was incomprehensible. Unrestrained shouting was interrupted by cheering. The din was loud and sustained. There were some swear words and then some ominous thumps. We learned later that Donnelly and the chairman, Cecil John (Neyland) had actually engaged in some sort of physical encounter and there was talk for a time of summonses for assault, but nothing came of it.

Osmonde John, the Llangwm Labour stalwart, told me afterwards: "Desmond and Rosemary (his wife) put up a desperate fight to get the support of the local Party but they didn't have a leg to stand on. But I didn't blame them - they were fighting for their lives". This was an accurate assessment, for the April 6th meeting was, in fact, the end of Desmond's political career. He put on a typically brave face afterwards and maintained it for a long time, but he was never again regarded as a formidable contender. The meeting broke up with the Labour Party loyalists walking out, leaving Desmond and his supporters in possession of Willie Jenkins' House. "They've deserted the place", said Donnelly, declaring that he intended to stay there. Long and complicated legal procedures followed, the outcome of which was that the Labour Party eventually resumed control and occupation of the premises, and Donnelly left to establish headquarters in Dark Street, Haverfordwest, for his new Democratic Party.

As the 1970 general election approached, Desmond continued to behave in his usual ebullient, confident way. But those close to him noticed changes. He resorted to subterfuges to draw attention to himself; when he attended functions he either arrived late or left early; during a Mayoral luncheon at the Market Hall, Haverfordwest, at which he was a guest but not a speaker, he ostentatiously left the table three times in order, he said, to telephone the House of Commons to find out the progress of some matter there; he said that he was taking up cricket again and produced photographs of himself practising at the nets at Lords. It was all a bit pathetic. His secretary-agent, Glyn Rees, told me that there were many rows behind the scenes. "He could be very difficult at times", said Glyn.

At the start of the 1970 election campaign Desmond hired a four berth cabin cruiser, the "Glitterwake", a tiny craft moored off Lawrenny, which, he said, he would use as a retreat "the same as Jack Kennedy used to do". One day during the "Glitterwake" period, he turned up at the "Guardian" office unshaven and wearing a huge white polo-neck jumper, jeans and white boots. This, I concluded, was the pirate image! The "Glitterwake" was regarded by everyone as a gimmick and it did nothing to help his campaign, even if it did fly the House of Commons pennant!

The "Guardian" suggested facetiously that he, wife Rosemary, agent Glyn Rees and secretary Penny Sime could be sunk in the "Glitterwake" and published the following lines:

> Cast off, cast off! We're putting to sea,
> Just Rosemary, Glyn, Penny and me,
> The wild wind blows, it grows so dark
> The nearing storm, will it sink our bark?
> Oh for an anchor in Westminister lee
> For Rosemary, Glyn, Penny and me.

Such was the strength of Donnelly's personality and widespread the belief in his abilities that at the time many people took his Democratic Party seriously. He rustled up a good deal of support, mostly from people who were disillusioned with the two main political parties. One who came to Haverfordwest to speak for him was Johnny Johnson, the famous Second World War flying ace, but Donnelly got into trouble when he suggested that Douglas Bader was also supporting the new Party. Bader denied it. In retrospect, the Democratic Party was an obvious non-starter. It was short of money and bedevilled by many weaknesses and contradictions: while Donnelly was in favour of the Common Market, one of his candidates, in Liverpool I think, was proclaiming himself "Your Anti-Common Market Candidate". The 1970 election adoption meetings, all on the same day, provided a clear indication of things to come. At Nick Edwards' meeting at the Gold Room, Market Hall, one could feel the optimism. It was the most enthusiastic Tory adoption meeting that I could remember. Over at Willie Jenkins' House, the new candidate, Gordon Parry, was also having a grand time with the Labour Party confident that it had now surmounted all its recent troubles. But when I hurried down to the Masonic Hall, where the Democrats were holding their meeting, I found not only a small attendance but no atmosphere at all. It was a depressing occasion. "We will form a Government in 1974". said Desmond with a touch of the old fire, but he couldn't have believed it. Nobody else did.

The Democrats contested five seats in the country without a single success and after the election the Party quickly disappeared. Desmond then confessed that it was only "a temporary umbrella" (this was misquoted in some quarters as "a leaky umbrella") and, after a short lapse of time, having left the county, he joined the Conservative Party in London. But his strenuous efforts to secure a Tory candidature were unsuccessful.

Desmond Donnelly's constant shift of loyalties was much criticised but his argument was that, in the nature of things, changes occur and should not be resisted unduly. He often proclaimed his favourite quotation to be Emerson's "A foolish consistency is the hobgoblin of little minds". He certainly changed a great deal himself - in his attitudes and beliefs, and in his personality. But he always had a presence, a charisma, which tended to save him even when he was at his most infuriating. When he died so tragically in April, 1974, Pembrokeshire people, his friends and political enemies alike, regarded it as a tremendously sad end to a career which had been outstandingly successful for so long and which had had the potential to reach the highest pinnacles.

CHAPTER NINE

SPREADING THE NEWS (1)

It was the best of times,
It was the worst of times,
It was an epoch of incredulity
- *Charles Dickens*

In the days when newsprint was cheap and the trade unions were still cutting their milk teeth, newspapers proliferated all over Britain. Even the smallest town had its broadsheet. In Pembrokeshire over the first half of this century no fewer than twelve weekly newspapers were produced at one time or another - three in Haverfordwest, two each in Pembroke Borough, Tenby, Fishguard and Milford Haven and one in Narberth, with a few free advertising sheets thrown in for good measure. It was regarded as a challenging and worthwhile enterprise, the prosperity of the national dailies no doubt acting as an irresistible spur but, alas, most of the local newspapers duly folded, mostly through lack of capital, competition and a failure to adapt to changing times. No doubt there were also people around who thought that producing a newspaper was straightforward and easy, whereas, in fact, it was (and still is) highly specialised work demanding special aptitudes, not to mention complete dedication to hard labour.

The three newspapers in Haverfordwest - the "Herald", Telegraph" and "Guardian" - all started as district newspapers but eventually achieved county wide circulation. They were pitched directly against each other and the competition was fierce. Eventually, the oldest of them, the "Herald", founded in 1844, ceased publication (in the late 1920's), leaving the "Telegraph" and the "Guardian" as the two county newspapers forever battling for supremacy. It is this part of local newspaper history which the writer proposes to cover in this chapter and the next - the origins of the two newpapers, the early struggles and changing fortunes, the near-closure of both papers at different times and, not least, the personalities of the two men whose shrewdness and professionalism enabled both publications to survive and prosper during and after the 1914 - 1918 war. I refer, of course, to Mr.J.W. Hammond, who was associated with the "Guardian" for many years before he acquired it in 1916, and

Mr. John Thomas, printer, journalist and scholar, who bought the struggling "Telegraph" in 1918 and through sheer hard slog laid the foundations for its proud position today as the largest weekly newspaper in Wales. It makes a fascinating story.

The "Telegraph", the older of the two newspapers, started in 1854 in a cloak-and-dagger atmosphere caused by strong political beliefs which were then (as now) producing feuds and feelings of deep intensity in Pembrokeshire. Apparently, the "Pembrokeshire Herald" was unashamedly Conservative and week by week gave favourable publicity to the Party and its M.P. for Haverfordwest, Mr. John Henry Philipps (later Sir John Henry Scourfield). The local Liberals, a powerful group, were at their wits end about this and towards the end of 1853 a series of secret meetings were held to decide on some positive action to end what was regarded as a most unfair position. The outcome was the founding of the "Haverfordwest and Milford Haven Telegraph" for the express purpose of showing up the political short-comings of the M.P. Printing machinery, nearly all of it secondhand and ancient, was hastily acquired and in February, 1854, the very first edition of the "Telegraph" appeared and it is worthy of note that it has appeared every single week since, a remarkable record. The "Telegraph" also remained faithful to the ideals of its birth by espousing the Liberal cause, at least up to the 1950's by which time Liberalism was no longer a great power in the land.

Four men were mainly reponsible for the founding of the "Telegraph" - Sir William Davies, Mr William Rees, Mr William Owen and Mr William Walters, all aldermen of the Borough and greatly respected. They became known as "The Four Williams". Men of repute and substance they may have been but they were also hard taskmasters. They appointed an editor, William Phillip Williams, and he was under strict instructions to attack the hated Tories on every possible occasion, and it was said if any issue ever appeared without such an attack the hapless Mr Williams was summoned before the formidable four to expain his dereliction of duty! But the day dawned when the formidable four became the frightened four! Anxious to please his bosses the editor went too far in his commentary one week with the result that the "Telegraph" was threatened with libel. The four owners hastily sold the newspaper rather than face a High Court judge and, perhaps, be mulcted in heavy damages.

The new owner was another prominent local gentleman, Mr William Lewis, who continued to use the old, hand-fed printing press and newsprint produced at the Prendergast paper mills. Despite many handicaps it was a good production, as extant early copies testify. Towards the end of the 1800's Mr Lewis was joined by his three sons, John, Fred and Charlie, and between them they built up a properous newspaper and general printing business. They were all slightly eccentric but were held in a good deal of affection, and Fred became widely known as a pioneer breeder of Sealyham dogs. In fact, he was always referred to locally either as "Fred Lewis the Telegraph" or "Fred Lewis, Sealyham". Upon his father's death, Fred succeeded to the editorship and became a man of considerable local influence, being a magistrate, a pioneer of the Golf Club and an outspoken member of several local bodies.

For reasons no longer clear, the "Telegraph" business began to decline during the First World War. Increased competition from the "Guardian", now owned by the resourceful Mr Hammond, no doubt had something to do with it. There were also, of course, difficulties created by the war and in addition, some disharmony occurred between the brothers. The upshot was that the whole business - newspaper, printing works, buildings and shop - was put on the market where it remained, with little interest being shown, until 1918. It was then bought for £900 by John Thomas, a local journalist, and the whole course of its history changed.

John Thomas was a remarkable man. Studious, shrewd, exceptionally hard working, curmudgeonly at times, ambitious and undoubtedly courageous, he was at the same time modest but proud of his humble beginnings. He was born in Hook in 1880, the youngest of five children and left the local school at fourteen to become an apprentice printer on the newspaper which he was eventually to own and edit for twenty five years, becoming one of the county's most powerful men and a Justice of the Peace to boot. He was a willing apprentice but it soon became clear that his interests and aptitudes were literary rather than mechanical In addition to studying shorthand in the evenings, he read prodigiously, quickly graduating from penny dreadfuls to the newspapers and then to the English classics, such as Thomas Hardy, Wordsworth and Browning. Frank Rowlands, who served his apprenticeship alongside him, told me that John always had a book hidden beneath the printer's case (an oblong frame with divisions for holding type) at which he worked. "He was a quiet chap who did his work satifactorily but he always found time to get his nose into a book" said Frank. "The other boys used to laugh, but in the end John was the the wise one". This was true, for John's avid reading paid off handsomely in later years when, as editor, his writing was recognised for its exceptionlly high literary standards. Douglas James in "The Story of Haverfordwest" wrote: "His (John's) penetrating analysis of a problem or situation, national or local, expressed in faultless English, was a marked and pleasant feature of his writing".

After a few years he was given his chance as a reporter and gained experience in Somerset and Montgomery before returning to Haverfordwest to join the editorial staff of the "Guardian", now burgeoning as a county newpaper under the editorship of Mr.Hammond on behalf of the owning partnership of Evans and Hammond. He became a shareholder in the "Guardian" and everything was progressing smoothly until one day in 1918 he calmly announced that he had bought the "Telegraph" holus bolus - to the consternation of everyone, especially Mr.Hammond! Later John confided to friends that the purchase price of £900 represented his life's savings acquired entirely from his linage activites. Linage, for the uninitiated, is the word used in the newspaper industry for part-time work undertaken by local journalists for the national dailies. It was (and is) a sideline followed by every local reporter worth his salt - with or without his editor's permission! - and there have been instances of linage income exceeding salary, albeit by the hardest graft!

The "Telegraph" was revolutionised under John Thomas' ownership. In ten years all the obsolete plant had been replaced by modern machinery, a good staff had been recruited and, most important, the circulation had more than doubled, with consequent increase in advertising and sales revenue. It wasn't done by magic but by sheer hard labour. In the early years, although he was the boss, John turned his hand to every job there was. He was reporter and sub-editor, he wrote the leaders, helped with the type setting and printing, engaged part-time district correspondents and edited their copy, read the proofs and looked after the book-keeping. He did everything except polish up the knocker on the big front door! His idea of a day off was to travel the county visiting newsagents to urge them to sell more "Telegraphs". For a long time he drew no salary, but lived on his linage income. One of his first actions after acquiring the newspaper was to change its name to the "Pembrokeshire Telegraph" and about ten years later in view of the widening circulation into adjoining counties, it became the "Western Telegaph".

In addition to producing stylish, well-informed leading articles, he started a provocative column of notes entitled "Between You and Me" and signed "John Haverford", the pseudonym by which he came known all over West Wales. At the top of the column in small type was the standing message - "I am in a place whereof I am demanded of conscience to speak the truth, and the truth, therefore, I speak, impugn it whoso list." He certainly spoke the truth according to his own lights and was often in hot water over his forthright comments on a wide variety of activities, including local government. Councillors respected the column and, indeed, some of them were petrified at the thought of John Haverford "having a go" at them. Even his old boss, Mr.Hammond, by now a leading public man, was not spared the whip-lash pen, but it must be said that he at least accepted it all philosophically.

John Thomas was fortunate in his staff. His head printer was Mr. A.G. Gooding, a patriarchal gentleman with a white beard who was highly intelligent and a fine craftsman, while his chief reporter was the inimitable Billy Jacks. William Thomas Jacks, a member of a well-known Haverfordwest family, left Haverfordwest Grammer School in 1914 and started work as a junior reporter on the "Pembrokeshire Herald". Just over two years later he was called up and became the youngest sergeant in the British army. After demobilisation, he joined the "Telegraph" and quickly established himself as a reporter of exceptional talents. He had a wide range of interests, was quick-witted and had a tremendous capacity for hard work speedily executed. As the years progressed, he developed a knowledge of Haverfordwest, its people and its affairs which was truly phenomenal. It was said that he knew so much about local government that he could report a Council meeting without attending it - an exaggeration, of course, but indicative of the high esteem in which he was held professionally. Like every good reporter, he could cover any event - sporting, social, agricultural, you name it - and the speed at which he produced his copy was remarkable, and it was always good, readable stuff. Regularly over many years he reported the meetings of Pembrokeshire County Council which started at 11 a.m. and usually went on to about 5 pm by which time, in addition to taking copious shorthand notes, he had written five or six columns of the speeches, complete with headlines etc ready for the printers, and sometimes, in addition, produced linage reports for the "Western Mail" and "Evening Post". It was an object lesson in weekly newspaper reporting. His sharp mind and exceptional local knowledge made him a person of influence who was consulted by public men on all sorts of matters. He gave them advice, wrote their speeches and election addresses and was always at work behind the scenes. The local set-up was his life and he never took holidays except for a weekend in Chester now and again. He never stopped and was never tired. His value to the "Telegraph" was incalculable.

I am sure that John Thomas appreciated Billy Jacks' worth but it didn't stop him from complaining occasionally and unjustifiably that his influence and activities were confined to Haverfordwest, adding inconsequentially "He can't even ride a bike". There was always a sort of love-hate relationship between John and his staff. On one occasion a young printer made a stupid error and John sacked him on the spot. "Go home, you are not fit to be working here" he said. Two days later the youth received a summons back to work, whereupon John asked rather plaintively where he had been. "But you sacked me sir" replied the youth. "You old fool, you know I didn't mean it" said John. "Return to your work at once". Lyn Thomas, a particularly bright young reporter from North Pembrokeshire, was one day out with John in his car and was directing him out of a cul-de-sac when he said "You can reverse back now, sir". John stopped the car, got out and gave his reporter a long lecture on tautology. "It was as if I had committed some terrible offence" Lyn told me. "But I never said 'Reverse back' ever again!"

The "Telegraph" staff man in North Pembrokeshire for many years was the veteran Robert Howarth who, one quiet day, decided to visit Haverfordwest just to keep in touch with head office. John Thomas gave him a cordial welcome, entertained him to a meal and bought him cigarettes. A few days later Robert was amazed to receive a letter from his boss in which he expressed surprise that he had considered it wise to spend a whole day away from his district! The South Pembrokeshire correspondent, Colin Warlow, had an even sharper reminder that his editor was no push-over. During the war Colin, a senior member of the staff, took on a part-time job as a Ministry fuel officer for the district, which he contrived to combine with his reporting duties. He told no one about the "moonlighting" although, in fact, it was important war work. One day he wrote to John Thomas suggesting an increase in salary in view of his long service, the increased cost of living, etc. and so on. He received a one-sentence reply - "Dear Mr. Warlow, The time is fast approaching when it will take a good man to hold down one job. Yours etc, John Thomas". The secretive Colin took a long time to get over that one!

On the morning of Friday, July 23,1943, the people of Haverfordwest were shocked to learn that John Thomas had died in his bed from a heart attack shortly before 5 am. He was 63. Although he had not enjoyed robust health - no doubt the result of the cruel work burden he had always imposed upon himself - his death was unexpected and it took Haverfordwest some time to realise that it had lost an exceptional businessman and editor, a fine descriptive writer and a truly unique personality.

CHAPTER TEN

SPREADING THE NEWS (2)

Thy friendship oft has made my heart
to ache:
Do be my enemy - for friendship's sake.
- *William Blake*

Unlike the "Telegraph," the "Guardian" was launched without the benefit of political backing. The first issue was published at a small printing works on the main street in Solva on a Spring day in 1861 - purely as a commercial enterprise. Many weekly newspapers were started around that period to cater for the rapidly increasing literacy of the working classes, and are still flourishing, but the "Guardian" is unique in that it is probably the only newspaper to be founded in a tiny village deep in the countryside of one of the most remote counties in Britain and which not only survived many early vicissitudes but, against all the odds, went on to great success. It was started as a family business and remained so up to 1994, one of the very few family newspapers left in Britain.

Who was the man with the vision, or perhaps only the zeal, to start this unlikely enterprise? He was no tycoon, no son of wealthy parents drawing a bow at a venture. He was, in a fact, John Williams, a humble printer who served his apprenticeship at the modest printing works which had served the village and district, including St. Davids, for many years. No doubt impressed by the success of the "Haverfordwest and Milford Telegraph" launched a few years earlier in the County Town, John decided that North Pembrokeshire needed a similar publication, and with the active support of his wife Martha (a daughter of Henry Whiteside, the designer of the first Smalls lighthouse), the first issue came to be published in the first week of April 1861. It was called "The Dewsland and Kemes Guardian".

Compared with the modern newspaper, it was an extraordinary affair. Mr. Williams had arranged for the supply from London of a four-page paper, three pages of which were already printed and containing London and national news, and the remaining page left blank to be filled with local news. This was the front page, printed at Solva, and it contained a few advertisements and various items about local happenings. The other three pages were a solid mass of small type, broken only by minuscule headlines, giving news from all over the country. There were no advertisements on these pages and one had to wonder about the economics of the enterprise. Selling at a penny could it be financially viable? It must also have been an arduous task to keep the business going. The news had to be collected and written, the advertisements canvassed, the type all set by hand and the newspaper run off on a hand-operated press, probably already an antiquated machine, and then distributed. Even with only one page to be filled locally, this represented a lot of work and, of course, Mr. Williams also had his general or jobbing printing business to run, which was very important as it probably represented his main source of income.

So perhaps it was not surprising that Mr. Williams died a few years after starting his newspaper. And that could well have been the end of the "Guardian" but for one thing - the courage and resourcefulness of his wife Martha. At a time when equality of the sexes had never been heard of (in Solva, anyway), she not only took over the business but developed it, and by 1869 the paper was being published under the bold title "The Dewsland and Kemes Guardian, Cardigan Reporter and Advertiser For Pembrokeshire and South Wales" and underneath were the proud words "Printed and Published by Martha W. Williams at her General Printing Office, Solva". There were still three pages of national and world news, including a column headed "Metropolitan Gossip", but the front page now contained items from Milford Haven, Pembroke Dock, Narberth, Cardigan, etc, and there were a few national as well as local advertisements. Evidently the newspaper had made progress with Martha at the helm - she was by all accounts an enterprising lady with a facile pen - but the circulation could not have been more than two to three thousand, even allowing for the fair sale which had developed in Haverfordwest. The day of publication, Saturday, and the price, one penny, remained unchanged. Surprisingly for a newspaper published deep in Welsh Pembrokeshire, the "Guardian" at that stage contained no Welsh language except for the slogan "Calon Wrth Calon" (Heart to Heart) which remained on the front page for more than forty years. David W. James (a former headmaster of St. Davids County School), in his book "St. Davids and Dewisland, A Social History" states that the earlier editions of the "Guardian" were "remarkably dry reading, in a style of language remarkably unsuitable for local reading". He goes on - "With the years more local news was included, correspondence columns grew, and chapel reports in Welsh, articles by Henry Evans and by J. Young Evans, and, later still, the influence of a newly appointed

Welsh editor from North Pembrokeshire, Brynach, poet, preacher, teacher, made it into a genuinely bilingual paper". Mr.James also refers to the "Guardian's" interest in archaeology which started in its early days with articles by various Welsh scholars and continued up to the 1930's when Francis Jones (later to become the Wales Herald Extraordinary) wrote a fascinating series entitled "The Pembrokeshire Antiquary".

The industrious Martha Williams had a son, Henry Whiteside Williams who was brought up in the business and, upon her death, took it over. Henry recognised that there could be no great future for the paper without expansion into the populous areas of Pembrokeshire and he introduced far-reaching changes. More printing machinery was acquired which enabled the paper at last to be produced entirely at Solva, and this led to an eight and sometimes ten page paper filled with local news and trade advertisements with many public, legal and auctioneers' notices. He wisely changed the title to "The Pembrokeshire County Guardian and Cardigan Reporter (late The Dewsland and Kemes Guardian)". The price remained at one penny. He also made another important decision - to appoint an experienced full-time journalist to represent the "Guardian" in Haverfordwest and Mid-Pembrokeshire generally. This, he felt, was necessary in view of the newspaper's steady expansion but Mr. Williams had another, more personal, reason for it - he was an epileptic and no doubt wanted a good man at his side in case of a emergency.

The move turned out to be crucial for the future of the newspaper, for the man appointed, Joseph William Hammond, was not only a competent journalist but also a shrewd, courageous businessman who, more than anybody, was responsible for the "Guardian's" eventual complete emergence from the backwaters as a struggling country concern to become one of the most progressive printing and publishing houses in South Wales. He was only 22 when he arrived in Haverfordwest on Portfield Fair day in 1894. It was raining and seething crowds had come into town for the fair and J.W., pushing his way along the streets, didn't expect to be staying long in this peculiar little town. But, in fact, he stayed for sixty years and became one of the town's leading citizens and a prominent county figure. Born in 1872 in the village of Hazelbury Bryan, in the heart of rural Dorset, the youngest of the five sons of Joseph Owen Hammond, the village postmaster, he was educated at the small market town of Sturminister Newton nearby and started his working life in the printing trade. He quickly graduated to journalism and had worked in his home county (where he had the memorable experience of reporting a speech by the great W.E. Gladstone) and then for about two years as a reporter on the "Bucks Free Press" at High Wycombe before moving west. He had all the attributes of a good newspaperman - the ability to turn out readable "copy" at speed, competent shorthand, a knowledge of printing techniques, a great interest in people and, most noticeably, abundant self-confidence. He was also a dedicated sportsman who excelled at all ball games. Soon after his arrival in Haverfordwest he was playing cricket and soccer for the town, refereeing, serving on various sports committees and encouraging clubs to instal billiards tables as a means of keeping young men out of the pubs. Later, he became one of Pembrokeshire's best golfers with a handicap of five which he retained until well past middle age. There were people, including some of his colleagues, who were inclined to sneer at his devotion to sport, suggesting that he gave more time to it than to his work, but the truth was that sport opened many doors for him which was later to help him enormously in his business. It also helped to keep him active and always supremely fit.

His first acquisition in Haverfordwest was a bicycle and he became a familiar figure as he pedalled round the town and district and down to Neyland and Milford Haven in the endless quest for local news. Once a week, and sometimes twice, he cycled all the way to Solva with his copy and then back again. The result of all this activity was soon to be seen in the "Guardian". The advertisements included big spreads by Haverfordwest and Pembroke Dock businesses and the news columns contained reports of Haverfordwest Sessions, Roose Sessions, long reports of County Council Committees, Town Council meetings and many Haverfordwest paragraphs, including obituaries etc. For the first time, too, there was sport coverage with a regular feature entitled "Football News and Notes" which was signed "Referee" (no prizes for guessing his identity!).

In 1906, mainly upon the urgings of Mr. Hammond, the "Guardian" office and printing works were moved to premises near the entrance to the Bridge Meadow in Haverfordwest, leaving just a branch office with a small amount of machinery at Solva. This, of course, was a major development but there were to be troubled times ahead even though the newspaper was growing steadily and, with more modern machinery, was being produced more quickly and efficiently. A notice on the front page at this period, claimed that the "Guardian" was "recognised as the only county newspaper". But a few months after the move to Haverfordwest, on January 2nd 1907, the respected owner of the newspaper, Henry Whiteside Williams, was found dead in bed at his lodgings at Lower Cambrian Place.

There was a bottle of chlorodyne at the bedside and this caused some speculation, but the truth was that he took chlorodyne fairly regularly because of his epilepsy and as a soporific and it appeared that he had taken too much on this occasion. He was 52 and left a widow and grown-up family.

After this tragedy the "Guardian" was aquired by six leading Haverfordwest businessmen who formed what they styled "The County Guardian Company". Apparently they were all extremely optimistic but, with little or no knowledge of the intricacies and nuances peculiar to the newspaper business, they were soon in trouble and by 1908 the Company was in liquidation. Fortunately, Mr. Hammond's friend, Mr. Levi Evans, came to the rescue. Appropriately a Solva man who had worked on the "Guardian" as a youth, Mr. Evans was now the owner of the "County Echo" newspaper and printing works which he had established at Fishguard with great success in 1893 after experience in the printing trade in Bridgend and Llanelli. He took over the "Guardian", paid off its creditors and ran the paper for nearly eight years in conjunction with Mr. Hammond. They traded as "Evans and Hammond" and not many people knew that, in fact, the "Hammond" in the partnership was J.W.'s wife, Mary Ann, he, apparently, being precluded for some reason connected with the liquidation.

Levi Evans left the day-to-day running of the "Guardian" to J.W. and early in 1916 decided to relinquish his interest in the paper. The reasons for this are not known but it is likely that the two friends decided amicably to split up, the "Guardian" to concentrate its circulation in the south of the county and the "Echo" in the north, thus dividing Pembrokeshire between them as far as newspapers were concerned. The resurgence of the "Telegraph," then in the doldrums, and competition from the ailing "Pembrokeshire Herald" were evidently not given much consideration! Whatever the position, J.W. Hammond secured the "Guardian" on reasonable terms and it is known that he gave his friend a verbal undertaking not to press sales in the north, a pledge he honoured until Levi's death in 1928. Thereafter the "Guardian" had its own full-time representative in Fishguard but it never really re-gained its original position as essentially a North Pembrokeshire newspaper. In fact, it became a South Pembrokeshire paper with Pembroke, Pembroke Dock and Milford Haven its main circulation areas. The Company of J.W. Hammond and Co, Ltd, was formed in February 1916, and two years later, in April 1918, the headquarters of the business was moved to 18, Market Street, where, for many years, a printing and stationery business had been carried on under the name "Caxton Works" by the late Mr. Ll. Brigstocke. This was a major acquisition by the Company which still continued to operate from the premises until 1994 when, to the regret of all, the much respected firm went into liquidation and the "Guardian" title was bought by the owners of the "Western Telegraph". For a long time, despite the war and its many restrictions, the newspaper had three editions covering the mid, south and north areas of the county, and the "Guardian" was so well established in Pembroke and Pembroke Dock that simultaneously with the move to Market Street a branch office with printing works was opened at 11, Dimond Street, Pembroke Dock. In April, 1920, the price went up to twopence (from a penny) and it was claimed that the circulation was now "well over 7,000". The 1920's saw steady growth with two editions added, for Milford Haven and West Carmarthen, and branch offices operating in Milford, Solva, Cardigan, Whitland, and, later, in Fishguard. The growth also led to the paper being re-named "The West Wales Guardian". It was recognised everywhere as a campaigning newspaper with an exceptional news coverage, and many strangers to the county expressed amazement at the high standards it achieved in an area so far removed from the highly-populated and more sophisticated parts of the country. Its reputation was built on sound, dependable journalism which carefully excluded sensationalism, gimmickry and the unsavoury.

It was in the twenties, too, that Mr. Hammond, his business now flourishing, set out on what was to become an extremely distinguished public career. He was elected to Haverfordwest Town Council and was four times Mayor of the Borough; became a Justice of the Peace and chairman of the Bench; an Honorary Freeman of the Borough; a County Alderman; the holder of the OBE and the president and generous supporter of a great many sporting organisations. Douglas James, the local historian, in his book "The Story of Haverfordwest" described Alderman Hammond as "our outstanding public man of this century". It is of interest to add that when he was appointed to the Commission of the Peace in 1925 it was as an "Independent" and not as a nominee of the Labour Party as many were to claim in later years. The confusion undoubtedly arose because the "Guardian," always politically independent, was scrupulous in giving the Labour Party publicity equal to that allowed other parrties. It gained a reputation in some quarters as "a Labour paper" which, in fact, was totally erroneous.

The keen rivalry between the "Guardian" and the "Telegraph"

also began in the early twenties. Although of similar backgrounds and training, John Thomas and J.W. Hammond were entirely different in personality and temperament. John was essentially a cautious man whereas J.W always made quick decisions and was ready to "have a go" at anything. John was serious and studious, devoting his time to running his business and reading the classics; J.W. read thrillers (Arsene Lupin was a favourite detective) and to a large extent allowed his business to run itself, as he often said. John went to chapel on Sundays; J.W. played golf. Each had a fair conceit of himself; as Mr. Lang, headmaster of the Grammar School, once roguishly commented to me "Mr. Hammond walks down Market Street as if he owns it and Mr.Thomas walks along Bridge Street as if he doesn't care who owns it". The association between them was old established and they had a healthy respect for each other, but by the twenties and thirties relationships had become somewhat strained due mainly to the annoyances and jealousies of business rivalry. But it must be emphasised that both remained courageous editors who ran first-class newspapers. J.W. was always downright, straight, opinionated and authoritative. His word was law at the "Guardian" and nobody ever challenged it. He was always addressed as "sir" and in his absence was referred to as "the boss", even by members of his family. His temperament was illustrated by his interest in motoring and the way he exemplified it. In the early 1900's he was one of Haverfordwest's first motor cyclists and after the war owned a series of secondhand cars, some of them lefthand drive. Then, in the twenties, came a beautiful new Buick, followed by a Rover and an unusual model of a Chrysler. After the second world war he owned an equally unusual Oldsmobile. They were all big cars and J.W. revelled in driving round the county at furious speeds while his passengers hung on in obvious apprehension, much to his amusement. Driving home from golf in Tenby he used to say to his companion, Canon J. Bowden Thomas, at Cannaston Bridge "J.B., you'll be having your tea in seven minutes" - and, mostly, the Canon was delivered at St. Mary's vicarage right on time!

  On one occasion, W.H. John of Solva, a staid gentleman who ran the "Guardian" printing works there after the newspaper moved in to Haverfordwest, accepted a lift into town with J.W. It was a hair-raising experience and when he got out by the Shire Hall, Mr.John said "Thank you for the lift, Mr. Hammond - but never again!" In 1938, J.W. was fined for careless driving at Dungleddy Sessions (Clarbeston Road) when a witness said he was coming down Arnolds Hill, like "a b------ madman!" The case attracted big headlines in the local newspapers, including the

"Guardian".

On Maundy Thursday, 1932, a few hours after the paper had been printed - early owing to Easter - a fire occurred in the "Guardian" printing works, causing extensive damage to machinery and part of the building. It was an anxious time for all associated with the business but, thanks to the kind assistance of other local newspaper firms, including the "Telegraph," the "Guardian" was able to publish the following week and the record of never missing an issue since its inception remained intact, as it does sixty years later. Out of the fire trauma came remarkable developments. New machinery had to be installed and in order to utilise its full potential the Company decided to start a new newspaper "The Swansea Guardian". At the time Swansea had no weekly paper and the "Swansea Guardian" therefore met a need. It was printed at Haverfordwest and sent to Swansea by the night train on Thursdays. Through prodigious efforts by management and staff, the new paper made steady progress and it was soon followed by another weekly, the "Morriston Echo" also printed and published in Haverfordwest and dispatched post haste to Morriston. These two enterprises caused endless comment in the newspaper world and were the subject of several complimentary articles in London trade and professional journals. But, alas, the 1939 war with its almost immediate restrictions, including newsprint, put an end to the Swansea project and soon, facing many other difficulties, the "Guardian" was struggling to cover Pembrokeshire alone. Most of the staff were called up for military service - for a period of nearly two years only one reporter and three or four printers were left - but the paper managed to maintain its high standards and particular attention was always paid to reporting the activities and welfare of local Servicemen and local Service organisations.

One sunny day in early September, 1954, J.W. Hammond went fishing at Cannaston Bridge - his favouite recreation in his later years. On the way home a few hours later, his car hit the hedge near Slebech and rolled over on to the road. Remarkably, Mr. Hammond was not seriously injured but he died a fortnight later from delayed shock, and Pembrokeshire thus lost a truly outstanding personality. The "Guardian" and his record of public work remained as a memorial to his exceptional qualities of leadership, resourcefulness, energy and ability.

J.W. Hammond with his powerful Chrysler saloon which, because of its distinctive lines, not to mention the speed at which it was driven, became one of the best known motors in Pembrokeshire. With Mr. Hammond in this 1939 photograph taken at Pendine are a very young Gerald Oliver (centre) and friend.

Author in his first car, a 1931 Morris Eight, which had a sunshine roof (leaky) and disc wheels. Picture dated 1937.

Ivor Gwynne was the first Labour candidate in Pembrokeshire (he came second in the 1918 Parliamentary election with 7,712 votes) but it was Willie Jenkins of Hoplas, Pembroke (above) who became a household name throughout West Wales. He was Labour's champion at five general elections in 1922, 1923, 1924, 1929 and 1935 and although never successful remained indefatigably cheerful and loyal to the cause. He was loved by political friends and foes.

The sedate frontage of Haverfordwest's old Grammar School in Dew Street, the centre of a prolonged controversy in the 1930's.

Desmond Louis Donnelly, Pembrokeshire's first Labour M.P., who held the office for twenty eventful years. He was aptly described as a human dynamo.

The Donnelly family during their heyday in Pembrokeshire.

Desmond, regarded as one of Britain's ablest M.P.'s, with wife Rosemary, daughter Elizabeth (left) and twins Redmond and Rosamund.

Mrs. Joan Higgon (Messrs. R.K. Lucas & Son) supervising a pay-out from the Haverfordwest Freemen's Fund in 1969, with Mr. Stephen Green, Chairman of the Trustees, in attendance. The pay-out at the time was £5 each and was popularly known as "A fistful of fivers".

Members of Perrots' Trust with the ancient Sir. John Perrot deed which was discovered in the cellar of 9, Victoria Place, the offices of R.K. Lucas & Son, by Haverfordwest historian Douglas James in 1964. The deed, dated 1580, was later handed to the County Record Office for safe keeping. In the picture are (left to right):- Stanley Lucas (Clerk to the Trustees), Douglas James, W.T. Jacks, John Harries (Mayor of Haverfordwest), Col. R.F. Foster and J.M. Bishop.

Alderman J.W. Hammond, O.B.E., J.P., leading public figure, sportsman and editor of the "Guardian" for nearly fifty years.

Sergeant J.W. Hammond shortly before he was commissioned Lieutenant Quarter Master in the Pembrokeshire Volunteers, 1917.

A Camrose "boy" who became one of the most influential public men in West Wales, Alderman Richard Stephen Wade, J.P. He farmed at Dunston Park, Camrose South, for many years and was also a partner in the firm of Evans, Roach & Co., Auctioneers & Estate Agents. Later he lived on the Dale Road, Haverfordwest.

The men who followed up and wrote the local news stories in former years.

A group of West Wales journalists photographed at a get-together at Cardigan in 1935. Among those pictured (from the left, standing) are Sylvan Howells, Haverfordwest. ("Western Telegraph"), Lloyd Phillips, Haverfordwest ("West Wales Guardian"), Trevor Thomas, Cardigan. ("Teifiside Advertiser"),Morwel Jones, Fishguard ("Guardian"), Bernard Jones, Haverfordwest ("Evening Post" Swansea), Tom Lloyd, Aberystwyth ("Western Mail"), Idwal Nicholls, Pembroke Dock ("Guardian"), Bill Richards, Haverfordwest ("Guardian"), Bill Paton, Haverfordwest ("Guardian"), Bill Emmerson, Fishguard ("County Echo"), Robert Howarth, Fishguard ("Telegraph"). Seated are Ted Davies, Haverfordwest ("Western Mail"), Ken Jones & Brinley Jones, Cardigan ("Teifiside Advertiser"), E.R. Evans, Cardiff ("Daily Express") and Harry Lewis, Carmathen ("Carmarthen Journal"). It is interesting to note that Ted Davies, Sylvan Howells & Bernard Jones went on to hold important positions in Fleet Street while Idwal Nicholls became a high ranking R.A.F. officer during the 1939 - 1945 war.

R.S. Lang, the man at the centre of the great Haverfordwest Grammar School row of 1933 - 1934. An Oxford graduate, Mr Lang was headmaster of the school from 1927 to 1958 and achieved many outstanding successes.

Billy Jacks (right), known to his colleagues as "the fastest pen in the west". William Thomas Jacks was for over forty years the "Western Telegraph" chief reporter and general editorial factotum and played a great part in that newspaper's steady growth. He was a gifted journalist with a prodigious output and became one of Haverfordwest's best known characters who had much influence in local affairs. In this photograph he is accompanied by the author, Bill Richards, and his wife, Linda, at the Pembrokeshire Police Ball in 1966.

John Thomas, the man who laid the foundations for the success of the "Western Telegraph", one of Wales' leading newspapers.

A prodigious worker, Mr. Thomas was the Pembrokeshire representative of several national newspapers, including the old "Daily Herald". He claimed to have made enough money from this work, known in the profession as "linage earnings", to buy the "Telegraph" in 1918.

Mrs. Constance Lloyd J.P., widow of John Thomas. Originally an employee, Mrs. Lloyd (nee Williams) joined the staff as a clerk straight from school at the age of thirteen, married Mr. Thomas in the twenties and was actively associated with the newspaper until her retirement.

Luton. 26/3/06

Mr J. Thomas was for some time associated with me in the editorial work of the Western Chronicle & allied papers. He took a keen & intelligent interest in his work, was able to write readable & sensible comments on local affairs, & proved to be one of the safest reporters I have known. He was particularly good at condensation, & though a verbatim writer, could always give an excellent report in shorter form. His character is above reproach; &, in short, I count him a man in all respects above the average.

W. Bowdring

A glowing testimonial for the 26 year old John Thomas.

Colonel Walter Barrett, the County Architect (centre) arriving at the Shire Hall, Haverfordwest on September 17th 1963, for the first day's hearing of committal proceedings against him alleging corruption. On his right is his solicitor, Mr. R. Ivor Rees, and an assistant, while on his left are three Journalists, Messrs Cliff Phillips, Swansea (Press Association), Bill Richards ("West Wales Guardian") and David Allen (B.B.C.). Col. Barrett was charged with local builder Cyril Rogers and both were acquitted at the subsequent trial at the Shire Hall.

A.G. Gooding, head printer at the "Telegraph" in the days when John Thomas was building the newspaper into an influential county organ. A skilled craftsman, Mr. Gooding was also closely associated with the development of local library services.

One of the most successful officers in the history of the old Pembrokeshire Police Force was Cecil Bonsall James, who rose to the rank of Deputy Chief Constable. Upon retirement he entered local government and served with distinction on Pembrokeshire Council and Haverfordwest Borough Council becoming Mayor in 1958 - 1959.

Victor Noott, schoolmaster, councillor and intellectual, whose wisdom and quick wit contributed much to the richness of life in Haverfordwest and district. He was headmaster of Johnston C.P. School and became a member of Haverfordwest Rural District Council and, later, of Haverfordwest Borough Council.

Walter Thorne of Studdolph, single minded councillor, shrewd magistrate and highly successful cattle breeder.

CHAPTER ELEVEN

TOO LITTLE, TOO LATE

> For want of a nail the shoe was lost;
> For want of a shoe the horse was lost;
> For want of a horse the rider was lost;
> For want of a rider the battle was lost.
> - *Benjamin Franklin*

At the time of writing there are hopes that Pembrokeshire will soon be restored to its former proud position as a county in its own right and as a self-governing entity freed from the constraints imposed by the twenty-year amalgamation with Carmarthenshire and Cardiganshire. The county of Dyfed, we are told, is coming to end, and few will regret it. Indeed, many must wonder how on earth we got ourselves into it in the early seventies, and a resume of the situation at that time might not come amiss. The rumblings of local government re-organisation had been going on for years before the final eruption leading to the creation of Dyfed. The trouble was that nobody seemed to want to know about it. As long ago as 1961 the Local Government Commission for Wales had put forward definite proposals, which included the abolition of Pembrokeshire's existing eleven Borough and District Councils, to be replaced by two Councils. But this scheme fell through and in the following years the matter was discussed by local Councils only occasionally, and then in a most desultory manner. To most Councils it was not a matter of urgency, while the members of the general public just couldn't have cared less. Towards the end of the sixties, however, the threat to the old-established and comfortable existing system became more real. A Government Working Party had at last submitted its report, which included recommendations for the abolition of the existing Welsh counties and drastic reductions in the number of Authorities. It was clear that big changes, including the elimination of Pembrokeshire were in the offing. Every councillor in Pembrokeshire must have known this but it seemed to me, as an onlooker with a grandstand seat, that most of them failed to face up to it squarely, apparently trying to persuade themselves that the threat didn't really exist. They knew it was there but still hoped it wasn't! It was reminiscent of Hughes Mearn's children's rhyme:

> As I was going up the stair
> I met a man who wasn't there;
> He wasn't there again today.
> I wish, I wish, he'd stay away.

Eventually, of course, the issue had to be met and the County Council took steps to try and save itself and the County of Pembroke. There were several suggestions but the main ideas were the retention of Pembrokeshire as a local government unit controlled by one Authority, or alternatively, the retention of the County but with two District Councils. The vacillation and confusion on these matters had to be seen to be believed. I remember attending a county conference on re-organisation at the Shire Hall when the then unfamiliar terms "unitary", "all-purpose", "two-tier", "one-tier" etc. were being bandied about, and it was quite obvious that many, if not most, of those present had no idea what it all meant. The County Council, in the end, did try to save Pembrokeshire but their efforts lacked cohesion and were much too late anyway. In addition, County Councils moves were bedevilled by the attitudes and actions of the District Councils which seemed to me to be saying all along "If we have to go, we'll make sure the County Council won't survive".

Haverfordwest RDC with its ear close to the ground as usual (Welsh Office ground, that is) decided very early to support the two-tier system with two districts for Pembrokeshire, and would not be budged from this. In fact, the RDC declined to take part in the County Council attempts to find some other solution to the problem and even refused to allow the chairman of the "Save Pembrokeshire Committee", the Hon. R. Hanning Philipps, to put the views of that body to the Council. Other District Councils followed the RDC lead and there were endless arguments and criticisms as between district and county. This internecine strife contributed largely to Pembrokeshire's defeat. The Haverfordwest RDC lobby for Dyfed and two district councils was strong and persistent. But its strength came from a comparatively small number of members and officials who had the ability to impose their views on the remainder of the council. I always felt that the members concerned should have known better. They included articulate men of education and discernment, who should have been proud of Pembrokeshire's identity and anxious to retain it. I just could not understand why they adopted an attitude which so plainly meant not only remote and more costly local government but the destruction of a unique county. I should add that two of the group, Mr. G.W. John and Mr.

V.T.Y. Noott (both schoolmasters), told me frankly many years later that they came to realise how wrong it was to have supported the creation of Dyfed.

While all the arguments continued, the local newspapers, especially the "Guardian", were warning readers about what was going on and especially about the dangers inherent in the amalgamation of Pembrokeshire, Carmarthenshire and Cardiganshire into one unit of local government. The "Guardian" pointed out over and over that Pembrokeshire was a unique county with its own culture and background which would not "mix" with the Welsh strongholds of Carmarthenshire and Cardiganshire. It stressed that costs would rocket and, in particular, that "the local" would be taken out of local government. But, as usual, the ratepayers - the people who pay for all the excesses of their rulers - could not be bothered to rustle up much interest in the matter. There was, of course, a great deal of grumbling subsequently about the cost of local government and about the Dyfed County Council being so remote and unsatisfactory, but in the late sixties few wanted to do anything to prevent it coming about. One interesting development was that the Pembrokeshire County Council eventually agreed to two districts for the Pembrokeshire area but to continue to press for the retention of the county as a unit - and Haverfordwest RDC at a special meeting agreed by a big majority to support this, thus reversing its previous decision. It was a complete change of attitude by the RDC and a blow to the Dyfed supporters, but in fact it made no difference to the outcome. The faceless Civil Servants had long ago decided the pattern which local government reform should take and nothing would change this no matter what local councils decided or, indeed, what Government was in power, which is why I am not at all impressed when, as happens from time to time, one political Party tries to blame another for the government or local government mess we are usually in.

The Save Pembrokeshire Committee put up a gallant last-ditch assault and there were high hopes at one stage that their efforts would succeed. I admired their efforts but thought the decision to employ a professional firm to conduct the campaign was a mistake, involving a large amount of unnecessary expenditure. Had the campaign started several years earlier there would have been time to whip up real enthusiasm and recruit support from every town and hamlet in Pembrokeshire for positive actions of various sorts. Admittedly it would have been difficult at the start, but given the right leadership the campaign could have swept West Wales, with who knows what different outcome. The voice of the people, if properly managed, is all powerful! As it was, it was a fairly tepid affair; never was the cry "too little and too late" more appropriate.

It is perhaps idle to speculate now, because the battle for Pembrokeshire was over (for twenty years at least) when the Government finally announced the new Wales set-up. Not only was Pembrokeshire finished then as a unit of government, as a separate entity and as an historic county, but its very name was now under serious threat. This should have been obvious to everybody. South Pembrokeshire District Council wisely and loyally adopted a name which perpetuated the old county, but their opposite numbers north of the haven could not be persuaded to do likewise. Instead, they adhered to the ridiculous "Preseli", which is not only spelt incorrectly but is a name unknown outside West Wales. Here again the sensible pleas for "North Pembrokeshire" fell on deaf ears. Then the Post Office, in the manner of monopolies, announced that if the name "Pembrokeshire" was used on mail there could be delays in the post. It had to be "Dyfed"! Among those who protested loudly at this Post Office ban on the use of "Pembrokeshire" were some of the members of Preseli Council who had voted against "North Pembrokeshire" as a name for their Authority! Talk about inconsistency! After a time, bowing to public pressure, the Post Office lifted the ban while Preseli Council changed its name to "Preseli Pembrokeshire". It took them a long time to see the light!

CHAPTER TWELVE

THE SHIRE HALL

He builded better than he knew;
The conscious stone to beauty grew.
   - Emerson

Week by week for 160 years the Shire Hall at the bottom of Haverfordwest's High Street has presented a pageant of Pembrokeshire life. Behind its big doors and Georgian frontage countless decisions vitally affecting the county's welfare have been taken, many a legal drama has been enacted and many unusual occurrences witnessed. Mostly, it is and always has been a place for serious business and powerful people, making it the most important of all Haverfordwest's old and interesting buildings. It was for years the centre of Pembrokeshire local government and, for much longer, the place where the mighty wheels of justice were seen to grind so remorselessly in the form of the old and formidable Courts of Assize and Quarter Sessions. The Crown Courts, which replaced the Assizes and Quarter Sessions, are still held there, as are the less important Magistrates' Courts, the County Courts, various tribunals etc.

Many people may be surprised to learn that in former years the Shire Hall was used as a place of entertainment where music hall events, concerts, flower and bird shows, exhibitions and meetings of all sorts were staged. For some of these occasions a moveable platform was erected over the well of the main hall and the general public crowded into the semi-circles of seats at the back. Thus it often happened that after a week of Assize Court sittings when heart-breaking sentences of imprisonment were handed down by fearsome High Court judges, the scene would change completely, sometimes overnight, and the places where the lawyers performed their solemn duties would be occupied by light-hearted entertainers, and laughter would replace tears in the serried ranks at the back!

The Shire Hall was built in 1835 to replace the Guildhall which stood at the top of High Street. The Guildhall had served the town and the county for many generations but by the 1830's was in a run-down condition and the records state that in August, 1834 the General Sessions of the Peace (Quarter Sessions) held a meeting at which consideration was given to the "insufficiency, inconvenience and deficiency" of the building. After much agonising, it was decided to proceed with the erection of a new Shire Hall, mainly for holding the Courts of Assize, Quarter Session and Petty Sessions, and it was ordered that the Mayor and a committee of magistrates be appointed to inquire into the matter of a suitable site and the costs of purchase and building. Several sites were considered, including those at Castle Bank, the Coach and Horses Inn in St. Mary Street (where the building was later renovated and used for many years as the Borough Council Chambers), ground near the New Bridge and two areas at the bottom of High Street where Short Row and the Quakers' Meeting House stood.

Without much delay, the site of the Quakers' Meeting House was selected, a wise choice having regard to its central location and the fact that, with a fairly large garden adjoining, it afforded ample space for a worthwhile building to be erected. A house at the front was also available and, with the lot purchased for just over a thousand pounds in January, 1835, the developers must have felt well pleased with themselves! In today's terminology, it was a prime site although there were some misgivings about the proximity of Short Row, a rather peculiar dwelling area comprising two very narrow streets known as "Back Short Row" and "Front Short Row" which stood at the bottom of High Street. These houses, built by Francis Fortune, a member of a noted local family known for philanthropic works, were occupied by "a miscellaneous lot of people, some possessed of means and others very poor" and presented something of a problem as they literally divided the bottom of High Street into two narrow streets running from the entrance to Hill Lane on to the Castle Square. However, the Short Row problem was soon to disappear for the building of the New Bridge under the provisions of an Act of 1835 led to improvements of the approach roads which included the demolition of Back and Front Short Row. A pebbled area in front of the Shire Hall remained for over a hundred years as a sort of reminder of Short Row but it was cleared for a an asphalt surface about 1960, after many protests that it was destroying a valuable link with ancient Haverfordwest.

The Shire Hall was built by direct labour to the design of Mr. William Owen who also superintended operations as "Inspector of Works". Mr. Owen, a well-known local personality and architect, was also responsible for the construction of the New Bridge two years later. He must have been extremely efficient for the main structure of the Shire Hall, built in sandstone from Somerset, was completed within a year at a total cost of just over £8,000. Details of costs are no longer available, but some items can be given from the old records :- Masons, £289; labourers, £150; stones, £306; bricks £29; carpenters £420; slates £68; lead, £233; plasterers £210; stonemasons, £216. Iron railings at the front erected two years later cost £100 while £150 was spent on furnishings. Heating presented something of a problem which was solved, temporarily anyway, by the purchase of two stoves!

When, exactly, the Shire Hall ceased to be used for entertainment is not known but the late Mr. C.B. James, one-time Deputy Chief Constable of Pembrokeshire, who died in the early 1970's, told the writer that he could remember the platform being erected for a concert when he was a boy. And no doubt some will recall a flitch trial being staged in the main hall in 1934, organised by Mr. Martin Jones, solicitor (son of Mr. and Mrs. Basil Jones, Old Bridge) and won by Mr. and Mrs. Victor Noott, who were later to live for many years at Johnston, where Mr. Noott was headmaster of the local school.

The old-time entertainers were no slouches when it came to hyping their advance publicity. In the early 1880's, Professor Duprez (he came to the Shire Hall several times) announced himself as "The Original Prestidigitateur and Eminent Humorist". He also promised "an Original Dark Seance By Electric Light", adding at the bottom of the poster "Door open 7.30, Commence 8, Carriages at 10.30". Another poster of the period modestly informed the public that "Col. Dyke Has The Honour To announce His Refined High-class Entertainment Entitled 'Make Life Happy'. It includes Magic; A Fairy Harp; Clairvoyance; Ventriloquism; The Christy Minstrels; and an Amusing Illusory Extravaganza Entitled 'John Buttercup In Two Pieces".

The name of Barger, long associated with the Welsh music hall, appeared regularly in Shire Hall publicity, Tom Barger being an extremely popular entertainer, presenting conjuring, comedy, mimicry ventriloquism, etc., etc. Dramatic entertainment was provided regularly by Welsh and English travelling companies and in 1879 the Original New York Female Christys appeared in a song and dance programme with instrumental solos. Other entertainment, in addition to the regular flower shows, bird shows, etc., included:-

J.T. Tute's Great Minstrels - "Special Engagement At Enormous Expense".

"The Wonderful Byrnes", concert and entertainment. Painting displays from the Royal Polytechnic Institute, London.

The Royal Comedy Drama Company consisting of twelve ladies and gentlemen form the principal London and provincial theatres, presenting high-class comedies and dramas.

Poetry readings.

Mr. Jolly Nash's Concert Company.

Messrs. Livermore Brothers Original Court Minstrels, a company of Negro artistes. Also on this bill was "Tiny Tim", who was only 33 inches tall and was described as the smallest song and dance artiste in America.

An exhibition of plans and maps of the Haverfordwest area.

In January, 1884, Lord Kensington was allowed the use of the hall "to address his constituents", while in July, 1896, a public meeting was called there by Mr. John Green "to consider the state of the New Bridge so as to adopt means to make it free from tolls". Permission was given for the holding of a series of entertainments during the winter season of 1870 - 71 for the purpose of raising funds for the building of a Masonic Hall in Haverfordwest. This followed a letter from the Hall Committee dated 11 October, 1870. Among the more unusual events at the Shire Hall was a meeting in December, 1883, to present the Lord Bishop of Llandaff with a testimonial, while in the following month there was a public meeting for the purpose of "advocating the claims of Aberystwyth College to a continuance of present Government grants".

Of all the entertainments staged at The Shire Hall in a period of about seventy years, the most extravagant claims must have been those made for Miss Christine Millie, who appeared there for two days in May, 1877. In the advance publicity, she was described as the "Two-headed

Nightingale," and as "the Eighth Wonder of the World whose two heads talked together in English, French and German!" It was claimed that she had "four arms and four feet which in one perfect body meet". Modesty being evidently in short supply, one poster stated that Miss Millie was "the most interesting and marvellous personage in existence. She sings most beautifully, dances most gracefully and will converse with any two people on two subjects at the same time".

Was this hyperbole justified? Did it live up to its advanced billing? Unfortunately, there is no record of the quality or the real nature of the show or of how it was received by the good folk of Haverfordwest, but undoubtedly today's sceptics and cynics will make a realistic assessment of it!

Over the years much refurbishment and some alterations and extensions have gone on at the Shire Hall but, basically, Mr. William Owen's lay-out remains unchanged, a tribute to his skill and foresight. For those who have never visited the Shire Hall - and there are many who consider it a place to be avoided! - a short description of its main features may be appropriate. The top door, in the main, was and still is used as the official entrance while the bottom one is for jurors and members of the general public. Facing the street on the ground floor are the judges' and magistrates' retiring room and the jury retiring room, where the fate of many a man has been decided. Counsel's robing room was also there for generations, but it has now been moved upstairs, which is considered by many to be much less convenient. The inner (main) hall is laid out in imposing style and compares more than favourably with similar buildings in some of the larger and allegedly more important cities and towns in Great Britain. It is spacious with a high dome of strengthened glass which allows a maximum of natural lighting, the dome being supported by six magnificent columns. A raised bench for the judiciary commands the whole of the hall and immediately in front of it, at a lower level, are places for the clerks etc. - the people who ensure that proceedings always run smoothly - and in front of them is a large table at which, for Assizes and Quarter Sessions (and now for Crown Court), counsel make an impressive sight wearing their wigs and gowns. Seating behind counsel is used by their instructing solicitors and immediately behind them is that dreaded place, the dock, which may be entered from the hall itself or from the cells below. The remainder of the hall is available to the public with seating for about 300 and there is also a walkway around the back which, although curtained off by huge hanging drapes (which enhance the acoustics and help keep the place warm), is much used as standing room on special occasions. On the left of the bench are rows of seats for the jury and the Press and, opposite, seats for witnesses, officials and special visitors. There are also seats on the first floor level overlooking the well of the Court from each side. That vitally important place, the witness box, is immediately in front of the bench to the right of chairman's big chair. Below the main hall are the cells, while upstairs was a large room where "a grand jury" used to sit to determine whether "a true bill" was returnable against those due to be charged at impending Assize. With the abolition of the Grand Jury system many years ago, the room was used for other purposes, mainly for County Council committee meetings, and it has now disappeared altogether, the space having been adapted for other purposes. There is also a Petty Sessions room upstairs which is used as a "second Court" to the main Magistrates' Court.

Many mementoes remain of the Shire Hall's importance over the years not only to Haverfordwest but to the whole of Pembrokeshire. Prominent in the main hall are the embossed coats of arms of Pembrokeshire and of Haverfordwest, the former presented by Sir John Owen, Bart, Lord Lieutenant of the County, in 1837, and the latter by Sir. R.B.P. Philipps, Bart., M.P., Lord Lieutenant of Haverfordwest, in the same year. There are several spectacular paintings around the hall of important figures of the past, while a number of plaques to the memory of more recent leaders overlook the well of the Court. These include, among several others, Sir. William Howell Walters of Haroldstone Hall, an original member of the County Council and Deputy chairman of Quarter Sessions who died in 1934; Sir. Charles Philipps, Picton Castle, High Sheriff, chairman of Quarter Sessions, chairman of County Council, etc. who died in 1924; Sir George Bevan Bowen; Sir Edward Marlay Samson; Sir Wilfrid Lewis, a Judge of the High Court; Sir. Evan D. Jones, Bart, of Pentower, Fishguard, an internationally known civil engineer, M.P. for Pembrokeshire 1918-22 and chairman of Pembrokeshire County Council in 1926. On the right-hand wall near the main entrance to the hall are reminders of more modern days - two photographs of County Council members and officials, the first taken in 1960 when Alderman Fred Phillips, Neyland, was chairman, and the second in 1971 when Alderman Richard Yolland, Milford Haven, was chairman.

After the last war the work of the courts increased steadily and in 1971 plans were prepared for an extension to the Shire Hall to meet the growing demands. It was a difficult scheme requiring a great deal of architectural ingenuity, but eventually the new room came into being as an integral part of the Shire Hall, situated behind the Lower Three Crowns inn, and it was soon in regular use as the main Magistrates' Court, leaving the big hall downstairs free for the Crown and County Courts.

From the early days there had been complaints that charges imposed for the use of the Shire Hall for concerts etc. were excessive and no doubt these resulted in some reduction in lettings. But it was the creation of the Pembrokeshire County Council in 1889 that led to the real changes in the use of the hall which soon became more a place for meetings (and, of course, Courts) than for public entertainment. As the County Council acquired ever-increasing powers, more and more committees and sub-committees were set-up, all the meetings of which were held at the Shire Hall. The County Council itself always met in the main hall, the proceedings often lasting for a whole day, and on Court days there were occasions when every room in the building, no matter how small, was in use. Indeed, after the last war when Foley House, Goat Street (named "Folly House" by Alderman J.R. Williams of Pembroke Dock) was purchased, County Council committees were held there as well, and for a time the local magistrates also held sittings there, although the premises were not at all convenient for Court work. The Shire Hall was also used for all sorts of public meetings, Coroner's inquests, public inquiries etc. Haverfordwest Rural District Council, set up in 1894, had various venues for its meetings over the years, including the big dining room at the old workhouse for a long period, but ended up at the Shire Hall until Cambria House came into use in 1967.

The re-organisation of local government in the early 1970's changed the main uses of the Shire Hall once more. Pembrokeshire County Council and all its committees disappeared with the creation of the new county of Dyfed, and Carmarthen became the main centre of local government. It was a revolutionary change, involving great loss of status, power and influence for the old County of Pembroke, but there was one other result - the Shire Hall reverted, in the main anyway, to the role for which it was built, that of accommodating the all-important Courts of Law. It is, indeed, a majestic building, inside and out, which is admired with something approaching awe by visitors to the town but, one feels, is not fully appreciated by residents who seem inclined to take it for granted.

CHAPTER THIRTEEN

THE ASSIZES AND QUARTER SESSIONS

Be not afraid of greatness: some men are born great,
some achieve greatness
and some have greatness thrust upon them
- *Shakespeare*

In its long history, Haverfordwest has been granted many privileges, among them that of being chosen as one of the sixty one Assize towns in England and Wales. Under the Assize system, which started in the twelfth century, High Court Judges were sent out from London "on circuit" to try serious criminal and civil cases at important centres in England. The judges, directly representing the monarchy, were given enormous powers and their progress throughout the country on the "circuits" which they had been allocated was accompanied by great pomp and ceremony, which was watched in awe by the law abiding and in trepidation by the law breakers. It was regarded as a highly successful system. But it was not until the early 19th century that moves were made to extend the Assizes to Wales which, up to then, had been served by courts known as the Great Sessions sitting twice a year in every Welsh shire. The proposal was strongly opposed by the Welsh Members of Parliament who felt they would be losing much influence and independence by the abolition of the Great Sessions, but in 1830 the change was made and fourteen Welsh towns were selected to form the Welsh and Chester circuit. These included Haverfordwest where the first Assize Court was held at the Guild Hall at the top of High Street on March, 8th, 1831. It was the start of a long tradition, Assize Courts being held in Haverfordwest twice to four times a year until, in turn, this system was also abolished under the Courts Act of 1971, to be replaced by the Crown Courts.

Haverfordwest was unique in that a statute of 1543 enacted that the town should also be a County in itself separate from the County of Pembroke and with its own Great Sessions. This meant that Haverfordwest had two Commissions, which were read at the opening of the Assizes, and two Sheriffs, the County Sheriff standing on the Judge's right and the Town Sheriff on his left. If, as frequently happened, there were no criminal cases to be tried from the Town and County of Haverfordwest the Town Sheriff would present a pair of white gloves to the Judge, who responded with a few words congratulating Haverfordwest and its townspeople on their good behaviour!

The presentation of the symbolic white gloves was only a part of the ceremonial attaching to the opening of the Assizes, the arrangements for which were the responsibility of the Under Sheriff for Pembrokeshire. This extremely important office was assumed after the 1939-45 war by Mr. Howell P. Williams, well-known local solicitor, and before that had been held by members of his family for about eighty years, a remarkable record. On his arrival, usually the night before in a reserved railway carriage, the Judge was met at the station by the High Sheriff, the Under Sheriff and other dignitaries, all formally attired, and was escorted to his lodgings which were provided at a local house considered suitable for so important a person. In the last fifty years or so of the Assizes the lodgings were at Picton Town House (Picton Place), at Willowood (Merlins Hill), Cresborough (The Rhos) and Scolton Manor. The owners were expected to vacate their premises completely for the duration of the Assizes, leaving the Judge and his staff in sole occupation, and this sometimes created such problems that difficulty was experienced in arranging appropriate lodgings. In the Judge's retinue were his clerk, his marshall, a butler and a cook. On the following morning before the opening of the Assizes the Judge, in scarlet robe and full-bottomed bell wig, attended St. Mary's Church, accompanied by the High Sheriff and his chaplain, the Under Sheriff, the Mayor and members of the Corporation, the Town Clerk and a number of "County" people. There was a guard of honour for the Judge from one of the military units stationed in Pembrokeshire and trumpeters sounded a fanfare as His Lordship arrived outside The Shire Hall from the church. Invariably, a large crowd gathered at the bottom of High Street to watch the pageantry.

After about ten minutes in his retiring room, the Judge and his attendants entered the main hall to take their places on the Bench. A hushed Court, usually filled to capacity, saw the assembled barristers, all bewigged and gowned, bow in unison to the Bench and then began the formal ceremony of opening the Assizes in the manner followed for so many generations. The Clerk of Assize, bowing, read in precise tones the ancient Commission of Assize, a lengthy scroll which began "All persons having anything to do before my Lords the Queen's Justices of Assize of Oyer Terminer and General Gaol Delivery for this County and Town and

County draw near and give your attendance. My Lords the Queen's Justices do strictly charge and command all persons to keep silence whilst Her Majesty's Commission of Assize is produced and read upon pain of imprisonment ....". This and the "greetings" and "commands" which followed, all couched in archaic terms, was strong traditional stuff and it undoubtedly created an atmosphere which gave people a real sense of the importance of the occasion. The formalities over, the Judge retired for a few minutes and upon his return, now wearing a smaller, more comfortable bob-tailed wig, the real work of the Court began. Guilty pleas were taken first and were usually quickly disposed of, to be followed by contested criminal cases and then by civil actions which could last for several days. Depending on the calendar of cases, the Assizes could last a day, a week or, as in the well-remembered "lime case" at Carmarthen several years ago, for over three months.

In over thirty years of reporting events at the Shire Hall I never lost a fascination for the opening of the Court of Assize and I felt that it was only there that one fully realised the majesty of the law of this country. When the Assizes were abolished under the 1971 Act a vital part of our way of life disappeared, and it has not been replaced. Not everyone held this view. There were those who were strongly of the opinion that the Court and all its panoply had become an anachronism and, in particular, there was criticism of the ceremonial on opening day, including the attendance of leading county residents who usually watched the proceedings for a few hours. A rather left-wing colleague of mine used to assert only half jokingly that it was reminiscent of Madame Defarge and her cronies sitting around the guillotine with their knitting, a comparison which I regarded as more than extreme as the good folk in the Shire Hall were in the main the guests of the High Sheriff who were just waiting to attend his luncheon traditionally held on the opening day. Perhaps in the middle of the twentieth century there was some validity in the criticisms but my own view is that the ceremonial helped to promote respect for the rule of law, which is something we could do with today. In addition, the power vested in the Judges, who were treated with a deference equalled only by that accorded royalty, gave them and their Courts a tremendous authority which no one dared assail. Nobody played fast and loose with the Judges of Assize, and the few who were foolish enough to try were soon made to realise who was boss! The Court of Assize was a model of efficiency, judicially and administratively. The Judges, formidable in demeanour and intellect, knew their business. In addition, the sixty one circuit towns in the country were provided with a splash of colour and reminded of their important history every time the Assize Judge arrived. Was there anything wrong with that?

Over the years most of the famous High Court Judges came in turn to Pembrokeshire and Haverfordwest Assizes. At the first Assizes in Haverfordwest in 1831 the Attorney General of the day appeared for the prosecution in the most important case on the list while in the early 1900's the Lord Chief Justice, Baron Alverstoke, presided at the Assizes and, incidentally, played a round of golf at the newly opened Haverfordwest golf course on the Racecourse. Later, there were visits from the much feared Mr.Justice Horace Avory, who was known as "The Acid Drop" or "The Hanging Judge" because of his alleged severity, and from other nationally known legal figures, such as Judges Darling (a misnomer according to some!), Rigby Swift, Bruce Charles, Devlin, Denning (later to become the controversial Master of the Rolls), Reginald Croom-Johnson, Wintringham Stable (who lived in Montgomeryshire), Byrne, Cassels, Hallett, Elwes, Talbot, Basil Nield, Ashworth, Barry, Sellers, Havers, Cusack, Oliver, Thesiger, Wilfrid Lewis (a Pembrokeshire man) and Edmund Davies, to mention just a few. The last named, before his elevation to the Bench, appeared regularly as counsel at Haverfordwest courts and enjoyed much popularity. In 1964, as Mr. Justice Edmund Davies, he presided over the "great train robbery" trial at Aylesbury, and he subsequently became Lord Justice Edmund Davies, the crowning achievement in a brilliant career followed with interest by many Pembrokeshire friends.

Another judge who became well-known in Pembrokeshire was Sir Owen Temple-Morris of Cardiff. He, too, first came to Haverfordwest as leading counsel, then for several years as County Court circuit judge and later as Commissioner of Assize. Downright and outspoken, sometimes painfully so, he was yet kindly and was held in high regard by everyone connected with the Court. As a former Member of Parliament (Nat. Con., Cardiff East) he knew the value of the Press. When he entered Court there was always a friendly nod for the reporters and upon the occasions when he gave a reserved judgement he made sure that copies were handed to the Press bench, sometimes before anyone else had them! At his last sitting as County Court Judge at Haverfordwest, he paid eloquent tribute to all those who had helped him in his difficult work, and the reporters were among the first mentioned! He said that the full and accurate reporting of the Pembrokeshire newspapers had been extremely valuable and much appreciated. For once, the Pembrokeshire reporters walked tall!.

I never saw a jovial High Court judge but most of them showed flashes of humour and were humane when they thought leniency was deserved. They were above the rank and file, remote and unapproachable, and there were good reasons for this, for it would never do for a judge to mix freely with people who might be appearing before him in Court. Mr. Justice Nield in his fascinating book "Farewell To The Assizes", illustrates this point with a true story of a young man who at Paddington tried to find a train seat in a reserved carriage. When told it was the judge's carriage the man fled - he was appearing before the judge the following morning at Taunton on a serious driving charge. It was inconceivable at the time that the day would come when judges would be interviewed by the Press and even appear on television.

The only judge in my experience who was never anything except icily austere was Mr. Justice Croom-Johnson. He ruled his Court with grim-faced severity, striking fear into the hearts of everyone present. Even members of the Press, who by tradition were allowed to move in and out of Court freely in pursuit of their business, were afraid to leave their seats. Once, while a witness was taking the oath, Police Inspector Glyn Williams, a most respected officer and later a Superintendent, whispered something to the person seated by him. This did not escape the judge's eagle eye and, rapping his gavel, he stopped the proceedings and told the Inspector severely that he should have known better and that if he, or anyone else, offended in this way again when a witness was taking the oath, he would be put outside! Later, the same day a young police officer was mercilessly cross-examined by the judge over a photograph he had produced in evidence, the point being that he could not say for certain that the photograph was, in fact, the one he had taken. No doubt the police officer was wrong in not being able strictly to prove the photograph, but everyone present felt that the judge had been far too severe on a young man who, after all, was acting on a superior's instructions. Not long after, the constable left the Police Force, having obtained a commission in the army, but whether it had anything to do with this incident is not known.

Mr. Justice Croom-Johnson was the judge who at Lewes Assizes ordered the noisy aircraft from a nearby aerodrome to be grounded while the Court was sitting and then, when the order was ignored, hauled the high-ranking station commander before him and threatened him with imprisonment for contempt! Yet we were told that when his old nanny called to see him during an Assize sitting he was extremely considerate and made a tremendous fuss of her.

Mr. Justice Charles was a different type. He was famous for his comments in divorce, breach of promise and such like cases and it was said that he looked forward to reading the reports of "his cases" in the "News of The World" each Sunday. He came to Haverfordwest several times and always made a point of renewing acquaintanceship with Rev. Arthur Baring Gould, Vicar of St. Martins', with whom he had been at University. I was assured more than once that when the Court work was done, these two would dress in unobtrusive lounge suits and visit a quiet pub somewhere to talk of former days. Mr. Justice Charles was a chain smoker and apparently was in the habit of holding a lighted cigarette beneath his robes when pre-court ceremonial was in progress. On one occasion- it was in Cardiff - he stopped to chat to someone and, momentarily forgetting himself, put the cigarette in his mouth. A High Court Judge wearing a long wig and full robes and smoking a cigarette in public was a most unusual sight, if not infra dig, and Press cameras duly clicked. But at the judge's request, the photograph was not published. I doubt that such consideration would be shown today!

One of the most humane judges who came to Haverfordwest was Mr. Justice Elwes, father of Polly Elwes, for many years a popular television personality. His kindliness and good humour made for a happy Assize, while some of his down-to-earth no-nonsense comments from the Bench surprised everyone in Court. Shortly after the last war a circuit judge at Haverfordwest - Mr. Justice Cassels I believe - had to deal with a case in which a report in the "West Wales Guardian" was called into question, and I was impressed by his sympathetic understanding of the position. I was told later that as a young man the judge had spent several years as a Fleet Street journalist. A most unusual thing happened during the Pembrokeshire Winter Assizes, in February, 1945 when Mr. Justice Hallett was the judge. The Assizes opened in wintry weather on a Thursday and the Court was still sitting the next day when a severe snowstorm hit West Wales. The judge rose at about 5.30 p.m. and the blizzard was at its height when he left by car for his lodgings, then at Willowood, Merlins Hill. The top of High Street was already impassable and the judge's car, with police escort, made its way along Dark Street and up Barn Street where, predictably, it was soon in trouble. After a while the judge said he would walk the steep part of the hill, which he did, accompanied by his car attendant, Mr. "Dipper" Williams of Dew Street, a well-known local personality. The judge was a tall man, well over six feet, while Dipper was of small stature, and a police officer who was present told me they made a most amusing sight as they moved off slowly and carefully through the snow, Dipper holding the judge's arm and swearing roundly at the conditions. At the top of the street the judge got back into the car and good progress was made until they reached the top of Merlins Hill. Here they were confronted with a solid mass of snow, which made it impossible for the car to continue. It was also impossible to locate exactly the raised footpath on the left-hand of the road or the turning into Willowood further down the hill.

"Never mind" said the judge cheerfully. "I'll walk from here. It isn't far". "Yes" said the irrepressible Dipper "you follow me, sir, and you'll be all right. I know this place like the back of my hand, sir" Dipper then made off towards the raised footpath, missed it and fell into the deep snow engulfing the road, and disappeared completely from sight. After a few moments he came out, covered in snow and arms flailing, and said to the judge, "Christ sir, it's like hell". Mr. Justice Hallett, hands on his hips, threw back his head and roared with laughter. Then they had another go and this time found the path, and eventually reached the judge's lodgings. The next morning it was found impossible to put the judge's car on the road and it was decided that the one case still on the list should be heard at Glamorgan Assizes. As far as is known, this was the only time in Haverfordwest's long history that one of HM Judges walked any part of the journey between Court and lodgings while sitting at Assizes.

On another occasion Mr. Justice Denning was involved in an usual incident at the end of the Assizes. As usual, a crowd had gathered outside the Shire Hall to watch his departure when their attention was diverted by a swarm of bees settling on the police car which was part of the judge's escort. As His Lordship was ready to leave, frantic - if careful! - efforts were made to remove the unwelcome visitors, but all to no avail. In the end the Judge, a practical man if ever there was one, decided to leave without the police escort, probably another "first". Eventually the bees were removed in a make-shift hive by Mr. D.C. Nicholson, Haverfordwest Rural Council Public Health Inspector who was also a bee-keeper. It is said that an even more bizarre incident occurred many years earlier, in about 1870, when a dog sneaked into the Shire Hall and made off with the judge's lunch, a pheasant which had been roasted to a turn! Apparently, in those days the judge was provided with luncheon in his retiring room and on this occasion the meal was ready and the table set out ready for the judge when the dog, no doubt attracted by the smell, crept past the two javelin men who were guarding the room, seized the pheasant and scarpered, to disappear down an alleyway on the other side of High Street.

It is not known whether the dog was later arraigned for grand larceny!

All sorts of cases were tried at the Pembrokeshire and Haverfordwest Assizes. Rebecca rioters were sentenced in the 1840's and many Pembrokeshire men - and women - were charged with such offences as sheep stealing, cattle rustling, horse stealing, fraud, forgery and grand larceny. Murder trials were rare. After the conviction of William Roblin at the Great Sessions at the Guildhall in 1821 and his hanging at the County gaol at the Castle, there was a lapse of well over a hundred years before Pembrokeshire's next murder trial. This occurred before Mr. Justice Denning shortly after the 1939-45 war when a Pole, Jan Stowkowski, was found guilty of shooting a fellow-countryman in the street in Milford Haven. The judge duly passed sentence but Stowkowski did not hang - the Home Secretary intervened and the accused was committed to Broadmoor. Two years later enormous interest was created by the trial before Mr. Justice Byrne of Albert Edward Jenkins in what became known as the Rosemarket clay-pit murder case. After a hearing lasting for several days, the jury found Jenkins guilty of murdering his landlord, William Henry Lllewellyn, and he paid the supreme penalty at Swansea gaol. Mr. Justice Byrne was a kindly, undemonstrative judge and I shall never forget that when it came to pronouncing the death sentence he was almost overcome by emotion. We learned later that it was his first murder trail.

With the abolition of the Assizes, provisions were made for serious crime to be dealt with by Crown Courts which were set up in various towns throughout the country. These new courts were to be served - and are served - by High Court judges in the more important areas and Circuit Judges in other areas. Carmarthen was designated as a High Court judge town but Haverfordwest had to be content with a Circuit Judge only. Many regarded this as unsatisfactory but, at least, it was better than the fate awaiting some former Assize towns which, the Act decreed, should be served by Magistrates' Courts only. These included Lampeter.

The immense changes embodied in the 1971 Act were made to secure greater efficiency in the administration of justice, necessitated by the steady increase in criminal business. Whether everything envisaged has been achieved is matter of opinion. Certainly, the pageantry has all gone and today the Crown Court circuit judge, whoever he might be, arrives in Haverfordwest in his own car, parks in a space reserved for him and walks into Court to conduct the cases without ceremony of any sort. After the new system had been in operation for a few years, a Crown Court judge drove into Haverfordwest and must have been rather surprised that a parking place was not kept for him. However, he managed to park and then walked to the Shire Hall where an even greater surprise awaited him - the place was deserted. It turned out that, for some reason, the Court had been adjourned and everyone informed - everyone, that is, except the judge! Such a blunder could not have happened under the Assize system, but suppose for a moment that it had . . . . Krakatoa!

The establishment of the Crown Courts meant that, in addition to the Assizes, the ancient Court of Quarter Sessions also disappeared. Quarter Sessions, as its name indicates, originally met four times a year and was second only to the Assizes in importance, dealing with all the serious criminal cases except those of murder and treason. These cases were committed for trial by the Petty Sessional Courts, and Quarter Sessions also heard appeals from the Lower Court and, in the old days, had a fairly extensive jurisdiction in a variety of matters, most of which eventually became the concern of local government bodies. Quarter Sessions consisted of local magistrates presided over by a chairman who was invariably an experienced practising member of the Bar.

For a great many years Haverfordwest as a Town and County, had its own Quarter Sessions but eventually this Court was absorbed into the Pembrokeshire Quarter Sessions which, with the unrelenting increase in serious criminal cases, came to meet far more frequently than the traditional four times a year. Among the many chairmen and deputy chairmen of Quarter Sessions sitting at Haverfordwest during the past century were Judge W.S. Owen, Sir William Howell Walters, H.G. Allen, Sir Charles Philipps, Sir Edward Marlay Samson, Sir Wilfrid Lewis, Owen Temple Morris (later Sir. Owen), Rowe Harding and J. Havard Evans. In 1950, Lord Merthyr of Hean Castle, Saundersfoot, a barrister and noted public figure, was appointed chairman of Pembrokeshire Quarter Sessions and he held the office with great distinction for over twenty years until his retirement on reaching the age limit. For eleven of those years, his deputy was Colonel G.T. Kelway of Cottesmore, Haverfordwest, whose appointment was unusual in that he was a solicitor rather than a barrister. The Merthyr-Kelway "partnership" was undoubtedly a great success, the Pembrokeshire Quarter Sessions enjoying a widespread reputation as an efficient, fair Court where justice was done and seen to be done. The two gentlemen presided more or less alternately and enjoyed equal respect. The only criticism of Lord Merthyr, a prodigious worker, was that he sat for too long. His Courts would go on all day and sometimes late into the evening when he would rise in time to catch the night train to London where he had numerous interests in his busy public life. On one occasion, a local newspaper, the "West Wales Guardian", published a critical article about this under the huge headline "Too Late My Lord". Matters improved a little after that but Lord Merthyr was still always anxious to get on with the work and would sit for hours without a break while counsel and others grumbled sotto voce with such remarks as "Doesn't this man have a bladder?" I remember Mr. Breuan Rees, the Milford-born barrister, rising late one afternoon, when everyone except the chairman was visibly wilting, and requesting a short adjournment. Lord Merthyr looked up in some surprise and asked "For what reason?" to which Mr. Rees replied with typical aplomb "Not to put too fine a point on it, My Lord, some of us would like a cup of tea". The adjournment was granted immediately but it was clear that His Lordship had not even thought of such a mundane thing as a cup of tea! It was not that he was unkind - far from it - but that he was completely absorbed in his duties. Colonel Kelway also undertook the chairmanship in a most dedicated manner but was somewhat more relaxed and regarded long and late sittings as inimical to the interests of justice. "No one is at his best when tired" he used to say, often quoting the example of High Court judges who seldom sat after about 4 p.m. Colonel Kelway was also sustained by a sense of humour unsuspected except by those who knew him well. He loved amusing stories about local personalities and told many jokes against the legal profession, often quoting Mr. Justice Cocklecarrot's dictum that "Justice must not only be seen to be done but seen to be believed" ("Mr. Justice Cocklecarrot" was the brain-child of journalist J.B. Morton who, under the nom-de-plume "Beachcomber" wrote a delightfully funny piece in the Daily Express for many years).

Trial by jury is one of the great corner-stones of the British legal system. It has existed for centuries and, overall, has worked well based on the splendid concept that every man is entitled to be tried by his peers. But, observed from close quarters, at the Assizes and Quarter Sessions, surprise was often expressed that it worked at all - not because of the system itself but mainly because, in Pembrokeshire anyway, the jurors were mostly people who had never seen the inside of a Court before. Unlike magistrates, lawyers, pressmen and officials, they were in completely unfamiliar surroundings and it was plain that some were apprehensive if not highly nervous about the important duties now before them. The first task of a juror, once called and accepted, in a criminal trial is to read aloud an oath from a card handed to him or her. It was a simply-worded oath - "I swear by Almighty God that I will well and truly try the several issues joined between Our Sovereign Lady the Queen and the prisoner at the bar and a true verdict give according to the evidence" - but it was amazing how many stumbled over the words; indeed, some failed completely to read the oath and were then called upon to repeat the words after the clerk. It did not make for an auspicious start to the proceedings and there were those who were critical of the jury system on this ground alone. Other more tolerant observers took the view that it was the jury's understanding of the case once they had settled down and their eventual decision which were the really important matters.

Quarter Sessions did not begin to compare with the Assizes in the matter of pomp and ceremonial on opening day. At Quarter Sessions all that happened was that everyone stood as the chairman came in, usually accompanied by two lay magistrates, and the Clerk of the Peace then addressed the void with the words "Oyez Oyez Oyez. Any persons having business to transact before this Court draw near and give your attention". The Court then got on with its work. There was always some amusement at the dignified figure of the Clerk of the Peace performing his "Oyez" duty, not least because this was the ancient word always used by the Town Crier in former days prior to his making announcements in the main streets of the town. And you could rest assured that no sooner had the Town Crier shouted "Oyez, Oyez Oyez" than some wit within earshot would shout back "Oh no"! It should be added that this never happened within the Court!

Quarter Sessions was an important local Court conducted with great dignity and efficiency right up to the time of its abolition. No doubt there were valid reasons for change and the introduction of the Crown Courts, but it is fairly safe to say that very few people locally wanted to say farewell to the Quarter Sessions.

CHAPTER FOURTEEN

THE LIGHTER SIDE

I may laugh when I like, counsel may laugh when I laugh, and no one else may laugh at all.
- *Mr. Justice Swift's dictum on laughter in Court.*

The expression "Laughter in Court" is well known. And so it should be. Because although a Court of law is a place where serious business is transacted, and a man may lose his liberty, it is also a place where humour is never far away. Much of it is spontaneous, perhaps a re-action to the anxieties of the matter in hand. Some of it is carefully contrived. Always it is a welcome relief and this is especially so when it comes from the Bench because it indicates that those holding power can't be so bad after all!

My first experience of laughter in Court was at Haverfordwest Sessions in the early thirties when Mr. Mortimer Thomas, the genial proprietor of the Hotel Mariners, was summoned for allowing his pet donkey to stray on St. David's Day. Mr. Thomas wrote to the Court apologising for the offence and stating "I think the donkey had gone for a leak" (sic). About the same time an important civil action, a real cause celebre over foreshore rights at Setlands, between Broad Haven and Little Haven, was heard at Pembrokeshire Assizes. In proceedings which went on for several days, one of the witnesses was Alderman Thomas Randle Dawkins, a well-remembered Pembrokeshire public figure and personality. When he entered the witness box, the following exchange ensued:-

Counsel: Will you give the Court your full name?

Witness: I am Thomas Randle Dawkins.

Counsel: And do you live at The Cottage, Little Haven?

Witness: No, I don't live there. I lodge there with my wife.

I remember thinking that it was a rather frivolous remark in such solemn surroundings but it sounded very funny, especially in Alderman

Dawkins' rather high-pitched voice, and even the Judge joined in the general laughter.

Some amusing Court incidents occurred in Pembroke Dock where for many years the Justices' Clerk was Mr. H.A. Jones Lloyd, a local solicitor. He was a man of impeccable character but was apt to talk a lot in Court and quiz witnesses, especially about their personal affairs. Once, a woman said in the witness box that she did not know who was the father of one of her several children.

> "What" asked Mr. Jones Lloyd with exaggerated incredulity. "Are you seriously telling the Court that you don't know who the father of this child is?"
>
> "No I don't" replied the woman. "It could be you, Mr. Jones Lloyd".

The Court rocked at this audacious remark and even the respected Justices' Clerk was quiet for a while!

Police Sergeant Charles Bodman, who was stationed at Haverfordwest for several years before transferring to Pembroke Dock, was a zealous but much criticised police officer. I'm sure that most people were unaware that he had a sense of humour which, if not sharp, was all his own. He used regularly to visit the "Guardian" office in Pembroke Dock where I then worked and we had a standing joke between us which was repeated practically every time we met. I would ask if there was much business for Saturday's Court (Pembroke Dock Sessions were always held on a Saturday at that time - and in the afternoon at that!), to which he would reply "Well, yes, we have one case of arson". I would express surprise that such an unusual case should be on the list, at which the Sergeant would produce the punch line - "Well, actually it's a case of arson about in Bush Street". He would then walk away chuckling hugely. A bit ridiculous, of course, but it helped to lighten the burdens of many a day.

Mr. F.E. Greathead, the Pembroke solicitor, was an able and unflappable professional man. He also had a great sense of humour. As a defence lawyer, he often had to cross-examine Sergeant Bodman and he did this relentlessly yet in a kindly sort of way. Many of his questions were in the nature of a leg-pull and I'm sure there was an understanding between the two men. Once, when Sergeant Bodman referred to someone as an expert witness, Mr. Greathead asked quietly "Now, tell me Sergeant, what is an expert?" Without hesitation, the Sergeant replied "An expert is a practical man who has also been to college". On another occasion when the Sergeant used the expression "without prejudice", Mr. Greathead, eyes twinkling, asked him what it meant. "It means no harm to anybody" replied the redoubtable officer. These were not too bad as spot answers! Sergeant Bodman was a valued and respected police officer, despite an undoubted keenness, and everyone was sorry when shortly after his retirement he was stricken by serious illness.

One day, a young woman defendant at Pembroke Dock - a "regular" at the Court - fainted while her case was in progress. Willing hands lifted her up to carry her out, in the course of which her skirt fell back on to her thighs. The women opened her eyes quickly pulled down her skirt and then resumed her "faint" and was duly carried outside. Alas, the drama failed to impress the magistrates. The lady was fined, as usual.

As indicated above, even the formidable Court of Assize was funny on occasions. It all depended on the Judge - some of the Judges did not go in very much for laughter when they were at work, but others didn't mind. I remember the following exchange in a case at the Pembrokeshire Assizes in, I think, the autumn of 1967:-

> Witness: He said we could nick it - sorry, I meant steal it.
>
> Counsel (Mr. Emlyn Hooson): If he said nick it, you say nick it.
>
> Mr. Justice Cusack: Yes, then we'll all be able to understand.

In the same case a witness was asked how he could remember that an offence in which he had taken part had occurred on a Wednesday evening and he replied "Well, we used to play darts every Wednesday, and I remember thinking that I would have to miss a match".

> The Judge: He remembered because there would be a clash in his engagements.

A few years later, Mr. Justice Talbot asked the jury mid-way through a case if they could be in Court the next morning at 10 a.m.

instead of 10.30 a.m. Immediately a little man stood up and said "It isn't convenient for me sir. I have to collect my dole at 10 o'clock"

The Judge: His what?

Counsel: He means he has to collect his unemployment assistance.

The Judge then arranged for the police to do the necessary collection and the Court re-started the next day at ten. An array of eminent counsel turned up at Haverfordwest for the Rosemarket murder trial, the leader for the Crown being Mr. W. Arthian Davies. Anxious to get everything right, I checked all their names and asked Mr. Davies "Do you use the W?"

"Only after breakfast" he replied crisply without looking up from his papers.

Even the prosaic County Court is sometimes enlivened by a little humour. I remember a defendant due to appear at Haverfordwest County Court sending a telegram which read "Unable to attend. Have broken my leg. Am sending by post." The Judge, His Honour Trevor Morgan, a most undemonstrative gentlemen in all respects, commented "When it arrives - C.O.D. no doubt - I'm sure the caretaker will know what to do with it".

On another occasion a painter and decorator told Judge Morgan at Haverfordwest that he had not worked for four months. Asked the reason, the man replied "I'm allergic to timber and paint".

An earnest and patently honest gentleman named Alexander Bowen created much diversion when he gave evidence in an appeal heard at Pembrokeshire Quarter Sessions in the early sixties. The appeal was by a Haverfordwest man against his conviction and sentence by Haverfordwest Magistrates for driving a bus in a manner dangerous to the public. His appeal was based on fresh evidence which, it was stated, had come to light after publication in the newspapers of the Magistrates' Court hearing. The appeal continued without much interest until Mr. Bowen's name was called and an elderly man limped into the Court carrying an attache case.

"This" announced Mr. Patrick Webster (barrister for the appellant) "is the fresh evidence", and a reporter commented, sotto voce, "It doesn't look very fresh to me."

Mr. Bowen gave an address in Carmarthenshire and he was then asked his occupation. Talking with a pronounced Welsh accent he replied "It's a poet and linguist I am, isn't it?"

Mr. Webster: But what do you do for a living?

Mr. Bowen: I can speak most of the known languages of Europe.

But you don't make your living at it? - Oh no, no.

What do you do for a living? - It's a small-holder I am. Yes, a small-holder.

Mr. Bowen then explained that he had seen the bus being driven on the day in question and in his opinion it was being properly driven. He had written to the driver after reading of his conviction in the newspaper. "My conscience compelled me" he declared. Repeatedly he told the Court he was a poet and then he quickly snapped open the attache case which was on the ledge of the witness box in front of him and produced a crown from it. He held up the crown with both hands and declared "I won this at the National". "Well done, Mr. Bowen, but you can put it away" said Mr. Webster tolerantly, and the crown-winner meekly obeyed. Cross-examined by Mr. Ben Oliver (for respondent) Mr. Bowen said he was hard of hearing but his eyesight was good.

Mr. Oliver: What was the colour of the bus?

"Ah" replied the witness "the colour - couleur in French, of course. No indeed, I can't say I remember the colour"

Mr. Oliver: I am not suggesting you are lying but that you are taking a bit of poetic licence.

Witness: I am here to help you to the best of my ability and to be friendly with you. I am here to speak the truth. I will not speak a lie for you or anyone else.

The Court dismissed the appeal against conviction but reduced a period of disqualification from six months to three months. It is interesting to add that the well-meaning Mr. Bowen with his attache case got right in to the main hall of the Shire Hall without let or hindrance. Had it happened a few years later when bomb scares had become rife, he would have been challenged at the front door.

To return to the Magistrates Court, a man appeared at Milford Haven to apply for a reduction in the amount of maintenance payable to his previous wife and when asked the reason for the application replied "I'm in the throes of getting married again".

Several years ago at Haverfordwest Court an Irishman was charged with assaulting his two-year-old son. His wife, who had reported the matter originally, now insisted that she should speak on his behalf. Given permission, she declared dramatically - "I want to say, sor, that me husband is after being a fine man. He is kind and good to me, sor. No better man ever stood on two legs, sor. But when he gets drunk, he's a bastard".

That splendid gentleman, Colonel Jack Higgon of Scolton, was chairman of Haverfordwest Bench for several years and brought to the Court much expertise, wisdom, understanding and humour. On one occasion an old and shabby man of the hobo type appeared before the Court for remand and, as he was of no fixed abode, the remand had to be in custody. But the old chap made a strong plea against custody. "Please don't send me in to prison again" he begged. Instead of arguing or pointing out the serious reasons for custody, Col. Higgon leaned over the Bench and said "But my dear chap, they have Dunlopillo mattresses and all in there now". The old man beamed and replied "Oh, all right then, sir" Remanded in custody for a week, he departed cheerfully and waved to the Bench as he went through the door. It was a classic example of how to deal humanely with an awkward situation.

On another occasion, Col. Higgon used the expression "amorphous agglomerate" from the Bench and, looking down at the Press bench, added "That will send the reporters scurrying for their dictionaries". It was intended as a joke, of course, but one reporter took exception to it and declared, sotto voce, that he knew as much about "amorphous agglomerate" as the Chairman, adding "I don't like being patronised by him". It is pleasing to record that Col. Higgon and the journalist later became firm friends. One Monday morning Col. Higgon amazed everybody by saying from the chair "You are a bloody fool" to a man who had been before the Court repeatedly - a sentiment which all agreed with but only the chairman could express. On another occasion he created quite a furore by telling a female defendant "You behaved very badly. There is a four letter word beginning with "s" to describe you but I won't say what it is". After the Court, everyone was asking what the four letter word beginning with "s" could possibly be, and a few days later the local newspapers were also asking the question. There were all sorts of suggestions, some of them none too respectable. Then a popular Sunday newspaper got hold of the story and its reporter, telephoning from Fleet Street, was more than a little miffed when Col. Higgon declined to solve the mystery, telling him "You are a man of the world. You guess". Months later, his shoulders shaking with laughter, he told his Bench colleagues that the word was "slag".

At a special Court at Haverfordwest Police Station one Saturday in the early eighties an attractive Spanish girl aged about 25 appeared in custody on a drugs-related charge. She was wearing a long dress of the flimsiest material. The magistrate remanded her in custody for the weekend but the young woman, with only a rudimentary knowledge of English, thought she was being ordered back to her homeland and in a flash she became a wild cat, screaming and dashing for the door. As two police officers restrained her, the flimsy dress slipped off to the floor to reveal not a stitch of clothing beneath! In her birthday suit she was hurried from the room, and the Justices' Clerk, the imperturbable Mr. James Eaton-Evans, turned to the magistrate and commented "Perks of the job I suppose".

CHAPTER FIFTEEN

AN UNCROWNED KING

He was a rapier disguised as a knobbly old walking stick.
- *Description applied to Sam Ervin, the American Chief Justice who dealt with the Watergate affair.*

A slightly stooped figure in a well-used trilby hat and mackintosh who walked with a limp and spoke in broad Pembrokeshire accents which he never ever tried to disguise - that was Alderman James John, Justice of the Peace, County and Rural councillor and un-crowned King of Llangwm, who was known throughout the county and particularly in Haverfordwest. Because of his modest demeanour many people under-estimated James John. They could not have made a greater mistake, and some of them lived to regret it.

James John came of humble Llangwm stock, who were working class and proud of it, and he had the minimum of formal education. But by the time he had reached middle-age he was a man of great local influence and went on from there to become one of the most extraordinary figures in Pembrokeshire public life. He wielded tremendous power, was feared by those who stepped out of line in any way, respected by most of his colleagues in public life, and held in affection by his close friends, of whom I counted myself fortunate to be one. In his native Llangwm and the surrounding area his popularity was unique. He was The Godfather (in the most benevolent way) and, indeed, scores of local people called him "Uncle Jim". This, I was assured, was not so much due to any filial bond as to the fact that in some way or other he had helped them along life's path. It was not just coincidence that so many Llangwm men and women held good jobs in public and other spheres! All this is not to say that Jim John did not have his opponents. They, too, were legion and no wonder when one considered that, when he felt the occasion demanded it, he was disconcertingly outspoken and a ruthless manipulator. The truth was that Jim John just didn't give a damn for anybody. He was completely without fear. He was never embarrassed by any situation or in awe of anyone's presence. Only once I saw him angry, and then he was very angry indeed. But even that lasted for just a short time. Sometimes when he had been particularly controversial I would warn him to be cautious. He always gave the same reply - "Why should I worry?" They can't sue me because I haven't got anything and they can't bribe me because I don't want anything". This, I believe, was absolutely true. He belonged to that extremely rare breed who genuinely have no interest in acquiring worldly wealth. He had no money or possessions, and this gave him more strength than the man striving for personal gain.

His courage was illustrated in many ways. When he was made a Justice of the Peace back in the twenties, he turned up at the Shire Hall for his first Court dressed in a jacket which had seen better days and a corduroy trousers. Having never been in the Shire Hall before, he stopped at the door and asked a senior police officer the way in. "Straight in through the passage" replied the officer brusquely, adding "And defendants sit at the back". There was a quick change of attitude when Jim said he was one of the new magistrates. Many years later I saw him stand his ground with remarkable tenacity in exchanges with Mr. Justice Wilfrid Lewis, a very well-known High Court judge who lived at Henllan, near Narberth, who was presiding over a Pembrokeshire Quarter Sessions business meeting of magistrates at the Shire Hall. These business meetings never took long; recommendations were explained briefly by the chairman and were then accepted with little or no discussion. There was, therefore, some consternation when James John rose before a full assembly to challenge a proposal that Major Hall Morgan, a fairly junior magistrate, should be appointed to fill a vacancy on the important Appeals Committee. Patiently, the Judge explained that it was a proper proposal and that the person recommended was fully qualified and suitable for the position. Normally, this would have ended any argument and clearly the meeting expected that it would on this occasion too. But Jim was not so easily put off. To everyone's astonishment, and to the embarrassment of some, he was on his feet again and said to the chairman "I don't accept what you say. There are many senior magistrates here and one of them should be appointed to fill this vacancy. It is not a job for an inexperienced magistrate". Some further exchanges ensued and the upshot was that the proposal was withdrawn and James John himself was appointed to fill the vacancy. I thought his acceptance of the office was a mistake. He should have proposed some other senior magistrate. But his courage in standing up to the top brass was admirable. Such things were just not done in those days.

When on the offensive, James John never gave in. On the defensive, he used every trick in the book and often "got away with murder" - without even being logical. I remember an occasion when some delicate matter concerning the Fire Service was due to come up at the County Council, and before the meeting members were saying that the Fire Brigade chairman (James John) was in for a rough passage. But when the moment arrived and a member got up and asked the awkward question - expected to be the prelude of a long discussion - the redoubtable member for Llangwm, without rising from his seat, replied "Don't be so quizzy" and the meeting, in an explosion of laughter, passed on to the next business. Behind the press seat, I heard a member mutter "My God, Jim's got away with it again".

The story is now well-known how Jim John scored repeatedly under cross-examination by two noted barristers, Mr. Hopkin Morris and Mr. Roderic Bowen, both MP's and Queen's Counsel to boot, at a public inquiry into the Pill Parks sport ground scheme. The inquiry was held in Llangwm, so Jim was on his own ground, and the hall was packed to the doors with locals, all rooting for him and expecting great things. They were not disappointed. Jim was on top form. To my ever-lasting regret I did not retain the full shorthand note I made of exchanges between the two eminent counsel and the local councillor. It would have made fascinating reading today! To every question, Jim John had a ready answer, not necessarily a relevant or logical answer, but one which appealed to the audience every time, if only because of the quick wit that was involved. It was a rare example of natural home-spun philosophy overcoming formal learning. Mr. Roderic Bowen, who was MP for Cardigan at the time, questioned him at length about Llangwm's contribution of £5,000 towards the scheme (a lot of money in those days) and it ended like this :-

> Counsel: And you say Llangwm could find this money?
>
> James John: Oh, yes.
>
> Without any trouble? - No trouble at all.
>
> Llangwm is a small village and £5,000 is a lot of money? - We'd find it easy. We're not in Cardigan y'know.

The room rocked with laughter at this sly dig at the Cardis' alleged meanness and Mr. Bowen flushed with anger.

James John's guile in fighting for things for his beloved Llangwm - houses, services, jobs etc. - was unbelievable. When a demand for, say, half-a-dozen Council houses for Llangwm was expected, the RDC would find him supporting a demand for some other area and even speaking, sometimes, in support of a member known to be antagonistic towards him. Those who didn't know him used to say "Old Jim must be slipping." I heard this phrase used more than once. What they didn't know was that "Old Jim" was just biding his time, waiting for more favourable conditions and gathering allies to his side so that eventually Llangwm would have a far better deal. I saw this sort of thing happen time and again. Jim was always thinking at least three moves ahead! Because he was so controversial, and sometimes outrageous, he always got a good press. He loved the publicity and made no bones about it, always making a point of thanking me when his activities got big headlines in what he called affectionately "the old Guardian". This was a welcome change, for most public men of my experience were equally keen on publicity but always pretended they didn't care about it and never said thank you when they got it. But he wasn't above trying to manoeuvre the press for his own purposes. At one time he was very keen on getting reporters to attend the meetings of Llangwm Parish Council. I told him it was impossible for staff reasons but he kept on about it and one day said: "The Telegraph are sending a reporter to Llangwm for Monday's meeting. I wouldn't like the old Guardian to miss out on anything". I then telephoned a friend on the Telegraph and asked if they were sending a reporter to Llangwm. "No" he replied "but Jim John told us the Guardian was sending one and he didn't want the old Telegraph to miss out on anything".

Jim John had a quick mind and a ready tongue. But he also knew when to remain silent. Once, at a County Education Committee he did something which greatly upset Mr. B.R. Lewis, the volatile member for Fishguard. After the meeting Mr. Lewis went for him on the steps outside the Shire Hall accusing him of humbug, hypocrisy, nepotism and goodness knows what else. The Fishguard man was really in high dudgeon. There were about a dozen councillors and others standing around and some feared it might even come to blows. But not a bit of it. Jim John just looked at his man with a half smile on his face, listened to the insults for a few minutes, then turned and walked down the street without uttering a single word! It was a classic lesson on how to get the better of an argument without opening your mouth.

He was particularly proud of being a magistrate and served

faithfully on the old Roose Bench. After the chairman, Alderman J.W. Hammond, resigned from office to go to Australia for a six-month holiday, Jim was confident of being elected to succeed him because he had been vice-chairman for some years. But when the Justices met to make the appointment, he had a shock. Alderman R.S. Wade was elected. I remember clearly the magistrates coming into Court after their meeting and, to everybody's amazement, Alderman Wade taking the chair, with Alderman John sitting beside him looking pale and visibly shaken. Jim told me afterwards - "I was taken completely by surprise. But I found out that Dick Wade had canvassed every single member of the Bench for their votes. The b----r ought to be shot".

During the last war and for some years afterwards, James John was the caretaker of the Masonic Hall, Haverfordwest, then used as offices by the Ministry of Agriculture. He had a room downstairs where all sorts of important people used to call to discuss Council and other affairs with him. Jim loved "holding court" in this way. But one day there was what he interpreted as an unpleasant occurrence involving the Deputy Chief Constable, Superintendent C.B. James. This was how Jim described it to me - "D'you know that C.B. James? Pig of a man. Came in to see me the other day with some summonses to sign. I said 'Good morning' but he didn't answer. He threw down the summonses on the desk and I signed them all, gave them back to him and off he goes. As he went out I said 'Good Morning' again but he didn't answer. He never said a word. So I went straight to the telephone and phoned the Chief Constable. I had a bit of trouble but eventually I got through to Evans (Mr. A.T.N. Evans, the Chief Constable). I told him what had happened and he said he was sure Mr. James didn't mean to be offensive and all that old rubbish. So I said 'Look here, Mr. Evans, please remember that I am one of His Majesty's Justices of the Peace and I will not have this sort of thing from you, your deputy or anybody else, so now you know how things stand'. I don't know what happened about it, but a week later I met C.B. James on the New Bridge and he gave me a magnificent salute and said 'Good morning sir''. In retrospect, Jim John was much amused by this incident. He certainly held no animosity towards Supt. James, whom he regarded as a very able police officer.

There were times when even James John's closest friends couldn't make out what he was getting at. I remember attending a meeting of Haverfordwest Grammar School Governors when, under "Any other Business" and completely out of the blue, he started asking questions about the school caretaker. What were the caretaker's exact duties? Was he expected to perform extra duties at times? Did he ever get overtime? And so on. The questions were answered and the meeting broke up with no explanation given as to what it was all about. A few days later I asked Jim about it.

"Why, don't you know? he said. "Old Lang (Mr. R.S. Lang, the headmaster) is keeping pigs at the back of the school and the caretaker is looking after them for him. I frightened him a bit I know, for after the meeting he followed me out and asked me to come to his study for a talk but I shrugged him off". Why Jim wished to get at the Headmaster in this indirect way I never found out. My guess is that he wanted a lever to get somebody a job on the Grammar School staff. What a man!

Two formidable ladies in local public affairs

Alderman Anne Norman (left), the only lady to become chairman of Pembrokeshire County Council, and Mrs. C.M. Cole, a leading member of Haverfordwest Borough and Town Council, and a former Mayor (twice), who later became a member and then Chairman of Preseli Pembrokeshire District Council.

Some of the personalities mentioned in this book are included in the above photograph taken upon the occasion of the opening flight of a scheduled air service between Haverfordwest and Cardiff by Cambrian Airways in May, 1952. Fourth from the left (front) is Alderman J.W. Hammond, owner and editor of the "West Wales Guardian" and then Chairman of Pembrokeshire County Council, and the two on his left are Mr. Ivor Male, Mayor of Haverfordwest and Mr. Jack Sheppard, Chairman of the County Council Aviation Committee. Also present are Mr. D. Tudor Hughes, Mayor of Tenby, Mr. J. Betty, Chairman of the Pembrokeshire Borough and District Councils Association and Mr. W.H. Uphill, Chairman of the Pembrokeshire branch of the National Farmers' Union. The two on the right (front) are Alun Williams, the noted B.B.C. personality and John Edwards, then a "West Wales Guardian" reporter who was later to become a prominent Fleet Street journalist. The others in the picture are Cardiff businessmen including (eighth from right) Mr. Frank Perry, father of Dr. C. Lynn Perry, the well known retired Haverfordwest general practitioner.

Members and chief officials of the progressive Haverfordwest Rural District Council photographed in the late 1960's during the chairmanship of Mr. Frank Sandall (Letterston), noted sportsman and a Burgess of Haverfordwest.

Four Haverfordians who over the years made a valued contibution to the welfare of the town and district as councillors and sportsmen.
Harold Arran (top left), George Jones (top right), Jack Evans (bottom left) and Stuart Hayden.

A family triumvirate! Top, James John, J.P., the "uncrowned king of Llangwm" and his two sons, Cecil John (left), schoolmaster, councillor and Labour Party stalwart, and Osmonde John O.B.E., County Councillor, Pembrokeshire representative on the Welsh Rugby Union for many years, and also a prominent member of the County Labour Party.

Sir. Hugh Thomas  Richard Knight Lucas

Stanley Lucas  Paul Lucas

A few of the stalwarts of R.K. Lucas & Son, Estate Agents, who have operated successfully in Haverfordwest under one name or another for over two hundred years. Bottom right is the present principal, Mr. Paul Lucas, who conducts the business in partnership with his mother, Mrs. Joan Higgon.

Lieut. Col. John Green, public figure and Master of the Gild of Freemen, an ancient and important body in Haverfordwest history (see Chapter Seventeen).

Freemen and Burgesses of Haverfordwest at their annual meeting in 1978. In the centre, front row, is Col. Jack Higgon, Master of the Gild, and on his left Col. John Green, who succeeded him in that office. A few years earlier, Col. Higgon had been mainly responsible for reviving the ancient Gild of Freemen, which now plays an important part in the life of the town.

CHAPTER SIXTEEN

ANY ADVANCE ON TWO HUNDRED?

Industry, brains, luck, influence -
a combination of any two of these ensures success.
- *An American Tycoon*

When most of Haverfordwest's great many old businesses have disappeared, as detailed in the 1992 book "Changing Face of Haverfordwest," it is gratifying to place on record that a few remain, still providing a valued service and contributing much to the general welfare of the town and district. One of these is R.K. Lucas and Son, surveyors, valuers, auctioneers and estate agents of the Tithe Exchange, 9, Victoria Place, Haverfordwest, which, under one name or another, has been in continuous operation for over two hundred years. Documents found in the firm's possession indicate that it was in business even before then - as far back as 1439 - but as no clear picture of those far-off days has emerged, 1789 has been taken as the year of establishment and the firm celebrated its bi-centenary during 1989, having survived many vicissitudes along the way.

The business has been traced back through the Lucases to the name of James Thomas and, before that, to the land agency of John Harvey and Sons who traded from Gloucester Place, Haverfordwest (1834) and, in turn, No 5 and then No 6, Victoria Place, from 1850 and 1884 respectively. It appears that John Harvey came to Haverfordwest in 1822, taking over as land agent to the estates of Lord Kensington, Colonel John Brooks of Noyadd (Cardigan) and the Bishop of St. David's. In this office he succeeded a gentleman named John Willy who, as land agent, managed part of the estates of Lord Kensington and the Bishop of St. Davids. John Willy's predecessors included Charles Hassall who, with a George Morris, prepared surveys and plans for the St. Davids diocese at the turn of the 19th century, and Henry John who, as a land surveyor, prepared plans for various estates throughout Pembrokeshire.

The earliest transaction of land with which John Harvey was directly associated was dated 12th February, 1789, and was between the

Rev. William Probyn and Zachariah Rogers and constituted a lease of land in the parish of Amroth. It was this document which provided a firm date for the establishment of the business although, as stated, there were clearly transactions going back over many years before then.

The business was continued by Harvey and his two sons, Richard and John, up towards the end of the 1800's when James Thomas, an employee of the firm, took over. He was an able and enterprising gentleman under whose direction the business, now known as James Thomas and Son, expanded steadily until it became one of the most important of its kind in South Wales, handling several large estates, including that of Sir Owen Henry Philipps Scourfield, Bart, one of the largest landowners in Pembrokeshire. Mr. Thomas, a local magistrate, lived in some style at Rock House, North Street, but also had a residence at The Dingle, Crundale, where Mrs. Thomas made her home for many years after he died in 1909.

If the business had been steadily successful under James Thomas and his predecessors, it became a spectacular affair after his death when it was taken over by his 29-year-old son, Hugh James Protherue Thomas, one of the most remarkable personalities ever produced by Haverfordwest. Already a junior partner with his father, he had shown remarkable enterprise in various successful property transactions in Aberdare and the South Wales industrial areas, and when he took charge of the firm he greatly extended his entrepreneurial activities, becoming an extremely well-known and respected figure. He had a meteoric career. At the age of twenty four he was elected a member of Haverfordwest Borough Council and served for many years, being Mayor in 1909-10 and again in 1918-19. He was also a County Councillor, a member of the District Council, a Justice of the Peace, a Governor of Haverfordwest Grammar School (of which he was an "old boy"), a Governor of the County Hospital, the Clerk to the Lieutenancy of Pembrokeshire, and held many other offices, including an active interest in sport (especially golf), agriculture, motoring etc. He owned the first car to be registered in Pembrokeshire, a 20 h.p. white Pieper (on December, 22nd, 1903) and his office had one of the first telephones in the town, the number being Haverfordwest 5. During the 1914-18 war he served as a commissioned officer in the army and in 1918 was awarded the O.B.E. in recognition of his work at the War Office. In 1922 he achieved his greatest honour, that of a knighthood in the King's Birthday list "in recognition of public services".

Despite his multifarious activities he continued to play an extremely active part in the affairs of James Thomas and Son and brought off several big deals in real property. Undoubtedly, the most remarkable, and probably the highlight of his astonishing business career, was the purchase of what was known as "the Milford Estate". This deal involved property to the value of about a quarter of a million pounds - phenomenal in those days! - and about a thousand householders in Milford Haven, Hakin and Hubberston, and also included several hundred acres of agricultural land adjoining. Also in the deal were the stately old mansion of Castle Hall, the Lordship of three mansions and the market tolls of the town. Sir Hugh gave an opportunity to all his tenants to purchase their freeholds and, despite tempting offers made to him, refused to depart from the principle of giving each tenant first refusal - a stand said to have been much appreciated by the people of Milford Haven. Then, in 1921, he presented the Market Square to the public of Milford Haven, freeing the town of tolls, to the great relief of the working classes.

After great expenditure on renovations and alterations, Sir Hugh took up residence at Castle Hall and lived there in the style of an exceptionally industrious country gentlemen. Alas, it was to not last for very long. In December, 1924, he was in poor health and, after Christmas, underwent surgery for appendicitis.. At first, all seemed well but complications set in, including pleurisy, and he died on December 30th, aged only 45. Tributes to his remarkable character, abilities and kindness poured in from all over South Wales and his funeral at St. Martins Church, Haverfordwest, followed by interment at St. Martins cemetery, City Road, was one of the largest ever seen in the County Town. A memorial service was later held at St. Katherine's church, Milford Haven, when it was reported that there was an "enormous congregation".

Sir Hugh's sudden death threw the business of James Thomas and Sons into some confusion but his executors were fortunate to have the services of two experienced gentlemen, Mr. R.K. Lucas and Mr. J.M. Simpson, who between them took over the management of the office. Richard Knight Lucas, a native of Burton who came to live in Haverfordwest at an early age, was already on the staff and had previously served with Messrs T. Rule Owen and Sons, estate agents, for many years. Soon after Sir. Hugh's death, Mr. Lucas took over the James Thomas and Son business, thus founding the firm of R.K. Lucas which became R.K. Lucas and Son after his death. Although of a quiet, reserved disposition, Mr. Lucas was an able businessman who took an interest in all public affairs, especially in matters relating to agriculture, with which he had been closely associated all his life. He conducted his business with marked success, becoming the agent for several large properties in Pembrokeshire, including the estates at Dale Castle, St. Botolphs, Langton, Moat and Williamston. The firm also became clerks to the Freemen of Haverfordwest, to the Sir. John Perrot Trust, Vawers and United Charities Trustees, Portfield Recreation Committee and the Prendergast Burial Board, with which his predecessors had been associated for very many years. Mr. Lucas died in November, 1943, after a short illness aged 77.

The period which followed, the war being at its height, was a difficult one for the firm. Mr. Lucas' only son, Mr. Charles Percy Lucas, was the County Council's Local Taxation Officer and was fully occupied in this important office, while Percy's son, Stanley, who, it was hoped, would succeed his grandfather in the business, was on active service in the Royal Air Force. Fortunately, the firm had a splendid staff and under Percy's general (if absent!) supervision, the business continued, Stanley taking over after his demobilisation at the end of 1945. The whole of Mid-Pembrokeshire heard with deep regret of the death of Percy Lucas in January, 1958, a year after retirement, at the age of 66. He was one of Haverfordwest's best known and best liked personalities, a forthright man with a refreshing sense of humour who, unostentatiously and anonymously, performed many kindnesses with no expectation of reward. Then, ten years later, the firm, not to mention the family, suffered another tremendous loss by the sudden death of Stanley Lucas. He had been working as usual on Wednesday, April 10th, 1968, but that evening complained of feeling a little unwell and a few hours later passed away. He was only 46. Like his father, he enjoyed the greatest popularity and was active in many spheres in Haverfordwest in addition to his conduct of the family business, in which he had proved a most worthy successor to his father and grandfather.

Once again, the business faced crisis. But, thanks to the resourcefulness of Stanley's family, the difficulties caused by his tragic death were gradually resolved. His wife Joan (nee Llewellyn of High Street, Neyland), with no previous practical experience, courageously took charge of the office and, with the assistance of professional friends, continued the business. In fact, the estate agency side expanded considerably in this period but the land agency began to decline due to the lack of qualified personnel. The appointments to the Charity Trusts also continued, Mrs Lucas receiving much personal support from the various bodies. In 1970, Mr. Desmond Reynolds of Ammanford, a Fellow of the Royal Institution of Chartered Surveyors, became a partner which led to considerable expansion and diversification of interests. In addition to normal transactions, notable events occurred in 1972, one of the most important of which was when R.K. Lucas and Son acted as joint agents with Messrs Jones and Llewellyn in the auction of the contents of Scolton country mansion on behalf of Lieut. Colonel J.H.V. Higgon, O.B.E., D.L.,J.P. Then in 1976 the firm negotiated the sale of land at Fenton Trading Estate, Haverfordwest, on behalf of the vendor, the well-known Mr. Jack Melville Bishop, for the sum of £270,000. The purchasers were Tesco, whose supermarket now stands on the site. A most interesting event in November of the same year was the marriage of Mrs. Joan Lucas to Lieut.-Colonel Higgon, one of Pembrokeshire's best-known personalities who, having sold Scolton Manor, had moved to a new bungalow at Ramshorn, Crundale.

Another important milestone was reached in October, 1977, when Paul Lucas, son of Stanley and Joan Lucas, joined the firm. Paul was a pupil at Haverfordwest Grammar School when his father died so tragically and went on to Reading University where he gained his Bachelor of Science degree in Estate Management in 1975. He spent the next two years with the Shropshire firm of Barber and Son, surveyors, valuers and estate agents, during which time he obtained his qualifications under the Royal Institution of Chartered Surveyors. He became a Fellow of the Institution in 1988. Thenceforward, the business was run by the partnership of Mrs. Higgon, Des Reynolds and Paul Lucas, and during this period the premises at 9, Victoria Place were given the name of The Tithe Exchange, in recognition of the many tithe transfers which had occurred there in former years. In March, 1990, Mr. Des Reynolds relinquished his partnership to become a consultant to the firm, his place being taken by Mr. Paul Griffiths of Saundersfoot, a well-known local sportsman who had been working as an assistant valuer for the firm for about four years following experience in the Estates Department of the London Borough of Hillingdon.

A long tradition was broken at the end of 1988, when upon a directive from the District Auditor the administration of the Prendergast Burial Authority (and that of the St. Martin's Authority) was transferred to Haverfordwest Town Council. This meant the termination of an association between Prendergast Burial Board and R.K. Lucas and Son, and the firm's predecessors, which went back for over a hundred years. With much regret, R.K. Lucas and Son retired from the clerkship and at the last meeting of the Board under the old regime high tributes were paid to the firm for its long and efficient service, special mention being made of Mr. Paul Lucas who had handled the Board's affairs in recent years. The Board decided unanimously to place on record its appreciation of his services.

In 1978, to facilitate the expanding influence of the firm, Paul Lucas opened a branch office at 36, Charles Street, Milford Haven, and when examining the deeds was pleasantly surprised to see that the premises formed part of the great property coup of his predecessor, Sir. Hugh Thomas, in the early 1920's. Another link with the past was provided in July, 1992, when R.K. Lucas and Son acted on behalf of a consortium of Pembrokeshire's businessmen in the sale of properties at the former Royal Navy Arms Depot at Blackbridge, Milford Haven. The properties included the historic gardens and grounds of Castle Hall where Sir Hugh Thomas had lived for a few years before his untimely death at the end of 1924.

Throughout 1989, R.K. Lucas and Son - one of the few family-run businesses left in the profession - celebrated its bi-centenary by sponsoring a number of charitable events in Pembrokeshire. This remarkable landmark in the firm's history happened to coincide with the silver jubilee of the Cystic Fibrosis Research Trust and the tenth anniversary of the formation of its Pembrokeshire branch, and R.K. Lucas' first celebration was to support events organised by the Trust, among other things donating 2,000 red and white balloons, the first batch of which were launched outside the Torch Theatre, Milford Haven, on January 25th, 1989. In March R.K. Lucas staged an intriguing show at The Queen's Function Centre, Haverfordwest illustrating 200 years of fashion. As the "Western Telegraph" reported "A large audience was taken on a quick trip back through time". This unusual event raised no less than £750 for the World-wide Fund For Nature. Upon R.K. Lucas' initiative an important visitor, Mr. Roddy Llewellyn, came to Pembrokeshire in May, 1989, to attend a grand summer ball at Wolfscastle Country Hotel (and, among other things, to visit Skomer Island). It was a highly successful event, a highlight of which was an auction conducted by Paul Lucas, the items offered including a Royal Doulton plate given by the Prince of Wales. It was sold for £770. The auction and its subsidiary events raised a total of £1,800 which was donated to Dyfed Wildlife Trust. Altogether, the Trust received a total of £3,000 as a result of functions organised by R.K. Lucas and Son to mark the bi-centenary year. The firm also took an active part in the organisation of the Tall Ships Race from Milford Haven in 1991 and, among other things, Paul Lucas conducted an auction at the Tall Ships Ball at Pembrokeshire College, which realised the useful sum of £1,645.

Today, in 1994, R.K. Lucas and Son is still a local family firm greatly respected throughout West Wales and providing a cheerful and efficient personal service. When consortiums and multiple concerns have taken over so much of business life everywhere, it is refreshing to know that a firm like R.K. Lucas has not only withstood the tribulations of two hundred years but still prospers in our midst and looks to the future with optimism and equanimity. Paul Lucas, endowed with a 200 year itch to get on with the job, says - "When people come to our offices, in Haverfordwest or Milford Haven, we assume that they require help and guidance through the quagmire of house and land affairs and we are there to offer personal help. With us, if you want to see the boss, you still can".

CHAPTER SEVENTEEN

A VICTORIAN RECORD

And now abideth faith, hope and charity, these three:
But the greatest of these is charity,
- *Corinthians*

Haverfordwest has many features which make it unique, among them the large number of charities and endowments from which its citizens have benefited for generations. In addition to the endowments which led to the founding and maintenance of the Grammar School and Tasker's School, Haverfordwest over the years from Tudor times had at least fifty charities resulting from bequests by its many prosperous merchants and landowners for the assistance of less fortunate inhabitants. Unfortunately, some of the charities gave rise to much public dissatisfaction, mostly because of alleged maladministration or neglect, and in the course of time many of them disappeared. One benefaction - it cannot strictly be called a charity - which remains and is well-known for its efficient and public-spirited administration, is that managed by the Freemen's Trustees and the Court of the Gild of Freemen. The history of the Freemen of Haverfordwest is so well documented that it scarcely needs repetition here, but an ancient record came into the author's possession recently which deals with the "Freemen's Fund or Portfield Money" in such an interesting, informative and amusing way that some of it, at least, is worth quoting.

This record is in the form of a small, slim booklet entitled "Haverfordwest Charities, With Numerous Interesting Local and Historical Notes and Useful Information". It is marked "Price Six Pence" with a line beneath stating "Will Be Forwarded Through Post For Seven Stamps". It bears no by-line or publishers' imprint although it is stated that the information was reprinted from the "Milford Haven Telegraph" and that the printer was W. Lewis, Bridge Street, Haverfordwest, whose family owned the "Telegraph" for many years. No date is given but as it is stated in the text that the Portfield Inclosure Act (1838) was "thirty-four or thirty-five years ago", it may be assumed that the booklet was published in the early 1870's. Set in the very small minion type-face and, therefore, a little difficult to read, the part dealing with the Freemen states in the somewhat archaic language of the period, that-

"The origin of this donation of a large tract of land on the south-western outskirts of the town of Haverfordwest, for the use and benefit for ever of the Poor Burgesses of the town, is lost in the remote antiquity of a long past period. Tradition, however, assigns it to the Benevolence of a member of the ancient Irish family of de la Poer (of which the Marquesses of Waterford are the head) who, in holy gratitude for preservation from imminent death during a very perilous passage from Ireland to Milford Haven, and in accordance with the devotional generosity more widely prevalent in former ages than in our own prosaic and utilitarian days, gave this property to assist the Poor Burgesses of Haverfordwest, with which place this family had been connected; and although that connection has long since ceased it may not be uninteresting to state that The Marquesses of Waterford actually take their seats with the House of Lords as Barons Tyrone of Haverfordwest, in the County of Pembroke. Some thirty years ago, the writer of this was shown by an elderly lady (the late Miss Argust of this town) an old title deed relating to certain property then belonging to her situate in Haverfordwest, and part of which was a dwelling house at the top of Hill Lane, described and mentioned in such deed as having belonged to the de la Poers. The old house was then occupied by Mr. Thomas Ellis, schoolmaster, and was a quaint and curiously shaped building, having a side porch in its front, and an extremely odd looking small round projection, in appearance resembling a miniature tower with a pointed roof. It adjoined the flight of steps leading from the lower part of Goat Street to Hill Lane, but was demolished some years ago, and its removal was undoubtedly an improvement to that part of the town; for in its then dilapidated state it was most certainly 'neither useful nor ornamental'. There were no means of ascertaining whether this house, in the days of its original dignity and greatness, had been the residence of some of the de la Poer family, but the presumption may not be unreasonably entertained that it had been at some long previous period; because so many Pembrokeshire men and families have settled in Ireland - even from the days of the conquest and subjugation of that country by Richard de Clare, Earl of Pembroke, known as Richard Strongbow, and his adventurous companions who sailed from Milford Haven - that there is scarcely an Irish family of distinction or note but at this very day trace their descent from Pembrokeshire ancestors".

Turning to Portfield, the article goes on - "It has been conjectured by many who have taken an interest in the subject that Portfield, as it is now called, might accidentally have been known as de la Poer's-field; afterwards became corrupted into Poorfield as it is often written in old documents; and then transformed into the more dignified and euphemistic appellation of Portfield. There is one genteel and comfortable dwelling house at the Dale Road, part of the reclaimed land, which the owner complimentarily named De la Poer Lodge, and thus, so far as in his power, perpetuated the original name of these lands. The property was for ages a vast furze and heath covered common, alike unproductive in its soil and sterile in its entire characteristics".

Referring to the Portfield Inclosure Act of 1838, obtained by the Mayor, Aldermen and Council of Haverfordwest in their corporate capacity, the article states that a large portion of the land was parcelled out under the supervision of John Wilson, barrister-at-law and Recorder of Carmarthen. "Such allotments" it says "were then sold to different persons:- The proceeds of such sales - after payment of expenses incurred - were applied in the formation of the new roads convenient to and over the lands; also the improvement of the then existing roads; and the enclosing, hedging and general utilisation of the unsold portions of the property, which are of very considerable extent, and on which there are several capital stone quarries; and here, also, are the reservoirs and works of the Board of Commissioners for supplying water to the inhabitants of the town. The unsold lands were divided into different lots and let on leases to respectable tenants for terms of twenty-one years, and lately for more extended terms, as farm and grazing occupancies. The land altogether is in a tolerably fair state of cultivation - although there is still plenty of room for improvement - and is what is known as extra parochial to St. Thomas's Haverfordwest. The race-course of somewhere about a mile and three-quarters in circumference contains a large area of land within its bounds, which was specifically reserved by the Act of Parliament to be for ever thereafter kept and used for the recreation of the inhabitants of the town and that it should be depastured by sheep only. The upper or northern portion of this area - formerly only entire waste land - is now undergoing vast improvement, being in a very promising state of incipient agricultural cultivation; and this is solely due to the energetic enterprise of John William Phillips, of this town, Esquire, who has spared no exertion or expense in the praiseworthy effort to reclaim and improve an extensive and useless piece of furzy and otherwise totally barren common, for ages the resort of a herd of half-starved horses, cows and donkeys. The lower or southern part of the area has been maintained partly as a cricket ground and for other recreative uses, and it is gratifying to find that several gentlemen of position and influence have formed themselves into a Committee and are now, perseveringly exerting themselves to improve the entire portion, so as that the inhabitants of the town may have the benefit of a Public Recreation Ground; and it is to be earnestly hoped that their efforts will be attended by liberal encouragement and success''.

The unknown writer goes on - "The annual income of the Portfield lands belonging to the Freemen is allowed to accumulate, and when it has attained to a sufficient amount it is paid in equal shares of forty shillings each on an average once every three years to all persons entitled to the rights and privileges of, and duly admitted and enrolled in open court before The Mayor, as Freemen of the Town and County of town of Haverfordwest. Those, however, who now possess such rights and privileges are not to be confounded with the poor Burgesses of the town for and to whom the gift was originally intended and made; because under almost all corporate charters, grants and regulations of old, there were three modes by which the Freedom, as it is termed, of a town, city or borough was obtained, and that was, firstly, by Birth (which meant being the son of one already enrolled as a freeman); secondly, by apprenticeship servitude (which was by serving an apprenticeship of seven years to a freeman who followed any trade but not one of the professions); and thirdly by prescription (which meant the nomination of a person by a member of the Common Council, and the appointment or election by that body of the person so nominated). This last has been discontinued either from the passing of the first Reform Act in 1831, or under the Municipal Corporation Act which came into operation on the 31st day of December, 1835. The designation 'Burgesses' has in the present day quite a different signification and meaning to that of 'Freemen' . . . . all household ratepayers are now styled 'Burgesses.' The present roll of Freemen of Haverfordwest shows the names of gentlemen of wealth and high position - even to the noble Earl - and strangers from different parts of England and Wales who could surely never have been intended by the donor of this

Charity to become participators in a gift made to the Poor Burgesses; but as all Freemen are entitled to a share of the money they do not hesitate to claim and receive it, too, just alike as do the poorest and neediest cobbler and tailor of the fraternity. To the lasting honour of some few of these gentlemen it should, nevertheless, be stated that their own private charities are great, indeed; whilst they, as well as some others, make a present of their share of the money to aid the funds of the Haverfordwest and Pembrokeshire Infirmary; and a more truly charitable application than this of their Forty shillings, not even the donor of the lands whence the money is derived could have desired".

The closing part of this old account is devoted to the "pastimes, revels and festivals" associated with the Portfield area in former days, including horse-racing which was "vigorously carried out" over three days and supported by the county families, and the "famed sports" always held at The Racecourse on Easter Monday. At the sports "fun and frolic once reigned supreme (interrupted occasionally by a bout of fisticuffs between some fiery rampant belligerents in whose brains the tincture of malt was operating untowardly)". There is also a reference to "Old Saint Cradock's Well, "the receptacle of hundreds of brass pins, which were dropped into its glassy waters in the expectation by those who made the offering, that they would see the reflection of some wished for face of absent relative, friend or lover, magically mirrored in its sparkling surface". All this, it says, is now done away with and the place just remains as a gloomy reminder "of days and funny scenes never again to return". Whit Mondays are described as "grandly important with the ancient associations of Civic greatness and dignity; when the Mayor, Aldermen, Common Council, Sheriff, Mace Bearers, and other Corporate and Town functionaries (after partaking of a magnificently sumptuous public breakfast, provided at the sole expense of the Sheriff of the town and county of the town for the time being) perambulated their boundaries mounted on richly caparisoned coursers".

"Portfield Gate Hiring" is described in some detail. It was, it states, "the long and anxiously looked-for-day of unbounded enjoyment and mirth, when 'Bobbies' had not made their unwelcome appearance on this terrestrial globe, and jovially inclined bucolic yeomen and farmers, with their comely spouses and handsome, bright-eyed, cherry-cheeked daughters, maidens not then corrupted by the fashionable frivolities of this very genteel age; but able, aye, and well used to carry the milking pail, churn butter, and phillit and press the cheese. Buxom ruddy-faced servant lads and lasses - the latter tricked out in rare finery and flaunting ribbons, were there in hundreds and hundreds, while our townsfolk of 'Honey Harfet' swelled the thousands who thronged to the place. Old and young, rich and poor, great and small, high and low, all, indeed, in that mostley and mirth-loving assemblage seemed to have fully determined on holding in veneration, for that day at least, the well-known lines slightly altered:-

'Begone dull care; I prithee begone from me,

Begone dull care; For thee and I shall disagree'.

"And who will not remember mine host of that old country inn - The Whale - who in those days had far more custom than himself and his many assistants could attend to; while the refreshment booths, the shows, swings, knock-em's-down, and other similar places were so largely patronised that their proprietors reaped a golden harvest, and the gooseberry, ginger-beer braggat and treacle tart vendors, and the nuts, cakes, gingerbread and other stalls transacted such roaring business that few, even if any, of our other country fairs could stand a comparison with it".

The Portfield Gate Fair, of course, was eventually moved to the open space at the top of Merlins Hill and then to St. Thomas Green, where it continues to be held on the same day as when it originated, 5th October. Incidentally, to this day the Freemen continue to maintain a tradition with the past by always holding their annual meeting, banquet and church service on the weekend nearest to Portfield Fair.

CHAPTER EIGHTEEN

ALL SAID AND DONE

Laugh and the world laughs
with you;
weep and you weep alone.
- *Ella Wheeler Wilcox*

Everyone who has had any association with public life will have noticed that occasionally people say and do the most extraordinary things, through inadvertence, ignorance or, in many instances, sheer cussedness. Journalists, privileged with a front seat at most events, notice and remember such things perhaps more than others, and this chapter is a record of just a few of the mistakes, malapropisms, idiosyncracies and instances of sharp wit which have caused amusement over the years. There is certainly no intention to jeer - we have all made too many mistakes for that! - but simply to stress that in all aspects of our life there is room for humour and good-natured laughter. Years ago, I am told, an old, gipsy was summoned at Llanelli Magistrates' Court for overloading his horse and cart, and he turned up to plead guilty, saying "Yes Your Worships, my cart was overloaded but it was all light stuff". That is the basis of this chapter - all light stuff!

Even the sharpest slip up occasionally as illustrated when John Nicholas was Mayor of Haverfordwest in 1931-32. John, managing director of Commerce House and a sharp man, mentally and physically, was presiding at a meeting at the Shire Hall where he had to introduce an extremely important visitor, Sir Thomas Inskip, K.C., famous lawyer, politician and a former Attorney General. The Mayor rose and, in his clipped tones, introduced him as "Sir Thomas Lipton" and then carried on oblivious of his mistake. Thomas Lipton was best known as a yachtsman.

* * * * * *

One of the leading educationists in Pembrokeshire in former years was Mr. George Jones, Milford Haven, a retired schoolmaster. Among his many offices, he was chairman of Milford Grammar School Governors and at the 1939 school prize day had the task of introducing the chief guest, Dame Sybil Thorndyke, the famous actress. To a crowded hall he said "Our chief guest is well-known to you all. She is a member of the oldest profession in the world". The audience received this gem in silence, the fifth and sixth formers kept straight faces and Dame Sybil said nothing. But a few weeks later in a speech in London she referred to this introduction with great glee. So it is plain, is it not, that even Homer nods!

* * * * * *

A well-known Haverfordwest character of the nineteen twenties and thirties was James Davies, a solicitor's clerk who lived in Portfield. He was known to everybody as "Jimmy Fine", for what reason no one knew except that Haverfordwest was always notorious for its nick-names. Jimmy fancied himself as a wit and leg-puller and could be quite rude, intentionally or not no one really knew. He used to visit the "Guardian" office regularly and always greeted the editor with "Good morning Mr.Hector Hammond, Ll. B., Barrister - at - Law, and how are you this fine day?" Mr.Hammond, a modest, down-to-earth man, always ignored the ostentatious salutation but Jimmy Fine was never put off. Mr.Victor Noott, well - remembered schoolmaster, councillor and raconteur, told me that one day he was travelling up the town in a bus when Jimmy Fine got in. "As soon as he saw me" said Mr. Noott "he stopped and exclaimed in a loud voice 'Ah, here we have Mr.Victor Terence Yardley Noott, Bachelor of Arts, a man who obtained a classical education at public expense.' For once, even I didn't know what to say or where to look". Jimmy also loved to make ponderous pronouncements which had no basis in fact. One morning he stopped me in Market Street and delivered himself of the following: "I think that as a young journalist you ought to know that there was once a prosperous businessman in High Street named White. When White died the business was taken over by a Chinaman whose name was Wong. But Wong was a waster and the business went through although his brother came down from London to try and help him. And that, my boy, proves conclusively that two Wongs will never make a White". Jimmy Fine, poker faced, then went on his way. He also always referred to the "Western Telegraph" as "The Penny Telegraph, Now Tuppence". This apparently, was harking back to the days when the newspaper was called the "Pembrokeshire Telegraph" and had recently changed its price form one penny to two pence.

* * * * * *

Next door to the "Guardian" office in Market Street was an ironmongers shop run by the well-known Herbert Family. It would be an exaggeration to say that there you could buy anything from a safety-pin to a traction engine, but I'm sure the family had aspirations in that direction! They sold just about everything and, when Woolworth's arrived offering articles at three pence and sixpence, Herbert's boldly went into competition offering their wide variety of goods at amazingly low prices. They continued this style of business for years and, stern individualists as they were, refused to conform when decimalization came in. Their window was still packed with items marked 3/11d., £1 -2s--6d and so on. The Herbert brothers' only shop assistant was a slight, beady-eyed man named Dickie Knight who, I think, lived in Church Street. He often took a break from his labours to visit the "Guardian" office and, as he came through the news room door, his greeting was always the same - "Hello, any news? Any vicar's daughters been foully done?" He always addressed Hector Hammond (the editor) as "Number One," Lloyd Phillips, my senior colleague, as "Swaff Senior" and me as "Swaff Junior". "Swaff" was a reference to Hannen Swaffer, a famous Fleet Street journalist for many years. Dickie was always friendly and genial outside his shop but when you went in there to make a purchase he became stand-offish as if doing you a favour. Like his employers, he was also an individualist.

* * * * * *

Local Council meetings deal with fairly weighty matters and, in the old days anyway, often became boring. But there was always a rich vein of humour not far beneath the surface and many a dull discussion was lightened by a quick witticism or some outrageous or ludicrous comment. In general, public men were tough and thick-skinned and did not mind being laughed at; in fact, they usually joined in the merriment, which tended to enhance their reputation. The old Haverfordwest Borough Council had its fair share of "characters". There was John White, a Dew Street butcher and an outspoken man who was never afraid to call a spade a bloody shovel, and frequently did. He was elected to the Council, second in the poll, in 1938 and soon gained a reputation as a fearless member. His favourite word was "typical" and often proposed a "typical" motion or amendment and once urged the Council to erect "a typical lamp" outside the Market Hall. One day I was walking along The Castle Square with my old editor, J.W. Hammond, when we met Jack White who straight away tackled J.W. about something which had appeared in the "West Wales Guardian". J.W. patiently explained that he was now retired and had no control over what went in or was left out of the "Guardian". Jack looked at him steadily and said "Can you see any green in my bloody eye, Mr. Hammond?"

Another personality was Ivor Male, who was always anxious that the Council should get on with the job whatever it was. There were delays in the Council's house-building programme after the war, the Town Clerk explaining on one occasion that there was a serious shortage of bricks, to which Ivor Male retorted "Never mind the bricks, let's get on with the houses". Walter Roberts was another member who always spoke his mind and took his duties as chairman of the Sanitary Committee very seriously indeed. He was never content at the full Council meeting to rise and say "I move the adoption of the Sanitary Committee report". Always he got up slowly and delivered himself of the following: "Mr. Mayor, sir, I move the adoption of the minutes of the Sanitary Committee as per typed and circulated". Members of the Council always waited for this little speech and seemed to breathe a sigh of relief when it was over! Walter Roberts enjoyed much popularity, on the Council and in the town.

After several unsuccessful attempts, D.J. Evans was elected to the Town Council in May, 1963. Known to everybody as "Dai Spit" (strictly in his absence, of course!), he was an extraordinary man, if only for his physical toughness (he lived to be over 90) and his complete imperviousness to criticism. He had more than a little conceit of himself and, although he never shone in the Council Chamber, he was inordinately proud of being a councillor. As recounted elsewhere in this narrative, he had a long-running feud with Alderman C.B. James, after he had reported him for a fairly trivial electoral offence, the matter ending up in Court. But at one Council meeting when C.B. made a strong plea for the retention of the Haverfordwest Shrievalty in the local government re-organisation proposals, D.J. Evans supported him, much to the surprise of everyone. C.B. James said "If we let this go (the Shrievalty) we will be selling our birthright for a mess of pottage". D.J. was on his feet at once and declared "I agree with the alderman. We would be selling our birthright for a pint of potash". Aldermen and councillors remained straight faced but C.B. James looked over at the reporters and raised his eyebrows almost imperceptibly.

* * * * * *

Although essentially a serious Authority, spending prodigious amounts of public money, the Pembrokeshire County Council always provided a leavening of light relief. At a meeting not long before its dissolution, in 1974, Osmonde John of Llangwm as chairman of the Neyland - Hobbs Point Ferry Sub-Committee was reporting on the position respecting the two ferry boats, "Cleddau King" and "Cleddau Queen", when he delivered himself of the following :-

"The Queen has gone into Milford Docks for an overhaul (laughter begins). The Queen is having attention but the King is back in service (increased laughter). On television it was stated that the Queen was stuck on a rock but we were having it off within an hour" (loud laughter).

The waggish J.R. Williams of Pembroke Dock then asked "Has the Queen been having her bottom scraped?" (uproar) to which Osmonde John replied, apparently rather crossly "I don't know what you are all laughing about. We are not talking about the monarchy but the ferry boats". Being the son of James John, the uncrowned King of Llangwm, Osmonde was something of a leg-puller and no one was quite sure whether or not he was being purposely ambiguous that day. Whichever way it was, he had the members in stitches.

At the same meeting, a member, upon being told that a certain decision could not be changed, exclaimed "My God, it is the law of the Medes and Prussians", while during a discussion of complaints about sewage discharge into the sea, an alderman commented "We must remember that every sewerage scheme in Pembrokeshire has been passed by members of the Planning Committee".

* * * * * *

Pembroke Borough Council, whose proccedings I reported for several years, was dominated at the time by one man, Alderman William James Gwilliam. He was educated, well read and, on the local scene, knew just about everything that was going on and he wielded his influence with tremendous force. He was proud of his gifts as an orator and, indeed, his command of words was formidable although he often made the mistake of being too learned and ponderous. He reminded me of Oliver Goldsmith's Village Schoolmaster:

"In arguing, too, the parson owned his skills,
For e'en though vanquished he could argue still;
While words of learned length and thundering sound
Amazed the gazing rustics ranged around;
And still they gazed and still the wonder grew
That one small head could carry all he knew".

Alderman Gwilliam never used a short word if he could think of a long one, and it wasn't often that he failed! When the two wards of Pembroke and Pembroke Dock were considering amalgamation, he was not content to say that the wards should sink their differences and get together. Instead, it was "We must terminate the continuous internecine strife which has so inhibited our progress and devise a scheme of rational contiguity" - the words rolling off his tongue with a relish he could scarcely conceal. He was on top form at a packed public meeting at Pembroke Dock Market Hall in January, 1939, called to protest at a proposed increase in the Town Clerk's salary. Referring to the Town Clerk's application for an increase, he declared "I should imagine that the Town Clerk's evil genius in the form of the Deputy Mayor was lurking stealthily at his elbow when he composed that document" - the Deputy Mayor being Councillor Denis Rees, then a somewhat controversial figure. The audience loved this and Alderman Gwilliam became more and more outspoken, going on to refer to "a mass of corruption" and "a state of affairs approaching Tammany Hall in this Borough". He also declared "We must cleanse the Augean Stables," which drew tremendous applause though I doubt that many present knew exactly what he was talking about. Incidentally, the protest meeting, which became so heated and seemed so important at the time, was all to no avail as the Borough Council at its next meeting approved the salary increase by a majority, although a bitter feud continued until the outbreak of war in the following September, when, with more important things to think about, the hard feelings were forgiven if not forgotten.

* * * * * *

A prominent member of Haverfordwest Golf Club told me that when his younger son was at infants' school he volunteered to sing a solo at assembly one morning. Two little girls, who had similarly volunteered, went in front of the class and , respectively, sang "Jesus Wants Me For A Sunbeam" and "Jesus Bids Us Shine". Then the young man marched out and sang "I've Got A Lovely Bunch Of Coconuts".

* * * * * *

"I think we should refer this matter to The Borough Survivor" - Cllr. Mrs. Mary Thomas (Haverfordwest's first woman Mayor).

* * * * * *

At the 1966 annual meeting of Pembrokeshire Agricultural Society at Haverfordwest complaints were made that the attendance figures at the annual show were greatly exaggerated. It looked like developing into an acrimonious discussion when president-elect Wilfred Davies (Lower Hoaten) said "Well, you know how it is. Somebody asks for the attendance figure and one of us climbs on to the roof of the secretary's office, takes a look around and says 'Oh about 20,000' and that becomes the official figure". End of discussion.

* * * * * *

Mr.Fred Thomas, one of the main organisers of an R.A.O.B. balloon race in aid of Pembrokeshire Blind Society funds at the 1967 Haverfordwest Festival Week, asked a number of passersby to buy a balloon but they all walked on unheeding. Commented Mr. Thomas - "This year we're doing it for the blind, next year we'll do it for the deaf".

* * * * * *

When I was reporting Neyland Urban Council meetings just before the last war, one member became conspicuous by his silence. In three years he never said a single word at any meeting which I attended. But often he would follow me out and say "Put me in the paper this week as saying something - it doesn't matter what it is as long as there is something there". He would then press a sixpenny piece into my hand and hurry off. Talk about bribing the Press!

* * * * * *

A much loved Prendergast character was Emlyn Hawkins of Coronation Avenue. At one period when he was unemployed Emlyn tramped the town and docks at Milford Haven looking for a job, with no success. At about his twentieth call, he was told "Sorry, we have nothing for you at present. Will you come back in the Spring?'' To which Emlyn replied indignantly "What do you think I am, a bloody cuckoo?"

* * * * * *

One of the great humorists on the Pembrokeshire agricultural scene in former days was Douglas Morris, the well-known Burton turkey breeder. He used to advertise his turkeys for sale in the local Press, adding a line at the bottom - "Phone Your Order Now, But Not During The News Or Tom And Jerry".

* * * * * *

On one occasion, reporters sat through a long meeting of Pembrokeshire Planning Committee without picking up a single line of "copy". When at last the meeting ended, the chairman, Alderman Idris Martin (St. Davids) said "Thank you, gentlemen, and thanks also to the reporters for being so tolerable".

* * * * *

On November 18, 1967, Pembrokeshire National Farmers' Union held a golden jubilee party in the Market Hall, Haverfordwest. The N.F.U. National President was due to attend but was prevented from doing so owing to restrictions on movement due to an outbreak of foot and mouth disease. The County M.P., Desmond Donnelly, then at a most controversial period in his career, took his place as guest speaker. I passed this information on to my colleague Derek Rees ("South Wales Evening Post"), adding facetiously "And Desmond hasn't got foot and mouth". Derek replied "Oh yes he has. Every time he opens his mouth he puts his foot in it".

* * * * * *

When an education psychologist lost his temper at a meeting of Pembrokeshire Education Committee, Alderman Hayden Williams (Narberth) turned to the Press and said in a stage whisper "These trick cyclists are all bloody mad".

* * * * * *

During the Royal visit to Pembrokeshire in 1955, members and officials of Haverfordwest Borough Council lined up at the Drill Hall to be presented to the Queen and the Duke of Edinburgh. When the Duke got to Willie Arthur Davies he shook hands, looked at him and commented "My word, what a fine sunburn you have". To which the irrepressible Willie Arthur replied "No, no , sir, that isn't sunburn, that's beer burn". The Duke was highly amused.

* * * * * *

One of the most popular members ever to serve on Haverfordwest Borough Council was John Harries of Prendergast. He was a councillor recognised for his sound common sense and as one who always enjoyed a little levity. When he was made Mayor in 1964, the ceremony was followed by the usual luncheon, and when it was all over and the Mayor's car was waiting outside the Masonic Hall, the Town Clerk (R. Ivor Rees) approached the new Chief Citizen, bowed and said with mock solemnity "Mr. Mayor, sir, your carriage is without". John, who was enjoying himself no end, replied "Without what, bloody wheels?"

* * * * * *

A pre-war police constable at Mathry, reporting that he had found a tramp asleep in the local church, warned his inspector - "Be very careful, sir, this man looks the very image of Jesus Christ".

* * * * * *

Once when a drugs case was being heard at Pembrokeshire Quarter Sessions, the drugs alleged to have been used - small black capsules - were produced and were given to members of the jury to examine. Eventually, all the evidence and addresses were finished, and the jury went to their retiring room. Half an hour later there was a stir at the retiring room door and my colleague Derek Rees hurried over to a senior Court official and said "The jury are at the door - they're asking for some more of those black sweets". For a split second the official looked alarmed - then realised he was having his leg pulled!

* * * * * *

John Burns, an assistant master at Haverfordwest Grammar School in the nineteen twenties and early thirties (see chapter five) was a well-liked local personality. Although a strict disciplinarian, he was popular with the boys mainly because his frequent admonitions were laced with an unusual brand of humour. In stentorian Scottish tones, he would order an offending boy to come out before the class, usually with the words "Come out you fool you" and then deliver a fearsome lecture which struck terror into the young man's heart, temporarily anyway. One day, he caught my friend, Alan Watt (Barn Street), busily at work carving his name into a desk with a pen-knife he had been given for Christmas. Thunders of Jove! "Alan Watt, carpenter and joiner, come out" he roared. Alan obeyed, of course, but was spared the lecture. Instead, he was sent straight to the headmaster for six of the best.

Like many a country boy, Ted Davies of Camrose, used to cycle to and from the Grammar School and in the evening do his homework on the kitchen table by the light of an oil lamp. One night his French paper got badly scorched as he dried it off over the lamp. He waited in trepidation the following morning as "Johnny" Burns was marking the homework. As expected, the call soon came. "Davies" the master bellowed "come out you fool you". As Ted stood in front of the class, "Johnny" waved the offending brown paper before him and shouted "Och mon, it was French I wanted not toast".

* * * * * *

Many years ago I wrote a leading article for the "Guardian" about local government re-organisation and suggested that, having regard to the changes taking place, certain procedures etc., could now well be discontinued. The heading on this leader was "No Longer Needed". A few hours before going to Press the printing foreman came to me to say there was no leader, that he was waiting for it and could I write it as quickly as possible. "I did it yesterday" I replied.

A search for the missing leader followed and eventually it was found that the youngest of the printing apprentices, having seen the headline "No Longer Needed," concluded that this applied to the leader itself and had thrown the type away!

* * * * * *

A local school teacher told me that several years ago he was counting dinner money in school, "assisted" by a boy of about eight, when a sixpenny piece fell to the floor. The little boy put his foot on it and the teacher said sternly "Foot off". "Foot off yourself, I saw it first" replied the boy - only "foot" wasn't exactly the word he used!

* * * * * *

The late Rev. J.C. Evans, a former minister of Bethesda, Haverfordwest, officiated at a wedding at the Tabernacle and, speaking at the wedding reception which followed gave this advice to the young couple: "Always remember this - it isn't the stork which brings the family but the lark in the night". The joke went down well but the bride's father professed to be extremely shocked.

* * * * * *

A home-made notice in a Haverfordwest chip shop in the 1960's read - "LEMONADE. If drunk on premises 4d. If took away 6d".

* * * * * *

Up to recent years, Haverfordwest was notorious for its nicknames which were applied wittily and with no disrespect towards the people concerned. Mr. Jim Llewellyn was known as "Kite" and Mr. Jack James as "Rough". One day, Mr. Llewellyn met Mr. James in Cambrian Place and called out "Good morning Mr. James, rough day". To which Mr. James replied "Yes, Mr. Llewellyn, too rough to fly a kite".

* * * * * *

Brigadier C.C. Parkman, a Liverpool consulting engineer, made a witty speech at a Precelly Water Board luncheon prior to the hand-over to the Pembrokeshire Water Board. I remember one of his comments - "Water and whisky are often allied but it is still as great a felony to make one in public as it is to make the other in private". Incidentally, Brigadier Parkman, being English, could never quite get his tongue round the name Llysyfran and always referred to the place as "Lizzie Fran".

* * * * * *

At a Pembrokeshire National Farmers Union meeting many years ago the chairman, a gentleman of most precise language and cultured accent, brought a discussion on cattle to a close and, studying the agenda, said "Gentlemen, the next item is the appointment of a shorthorn typist".

* * * * * *

George Jenkins of Monkton, Pembroke, farmer and sportsman, was an outspoken, down-to-earth member of the old Pembroke Borough Council. Once when the Borough Surveyor applied for a salary increase, one of several such applications, George exclaimed at a full Council meeting "I don't agree with this. Sack the b----r and have another". But he received little support and the Surveyor duly got his rise.

* * * * * *

Dr. A.B. Davies, a brilliant Haverfordwest surgeon and general practitioner, was giving evidence in an important case at Pembrokeshire Assizes and was still in the witness box when the Court rose for the luncheon adjournment. When proceedings resumed there was a long delay while a police car hurried off in search of Dr. Davies who had failed to re-appear. When, eventually, he turned up counsel gravely apologised for the delay, explaining that the doctor had been called to an emergency at the hospital. The Judge accepted this without comment. But the police car driver told me later that he had found the good doctor fast asleep on the couch at his home.

* * * * * *

A journalist colleague told me many years ago that a friend of his living in the Portfield area on the outskirts of Haverfordwest had an ornamental pool in his garden which was visited almost daily by a duck from a neighbouring farm The duck used to swim around happily for a while and then waddle back home. One day, the owner turned off the water and cleaned out the pool but was unable to finish the job. The following morning, the duck arrived, dived into the empty pool and knocked itself out. It recovered after a few minutes, staggered off and was never seen again.

* * * * * *

Superintendent C.B. James of Haverfordwest became one of Pembrokeshire's best known police officers. During a period when he was stationed in Goodwick, he was persuaded by local journalist-photographer Robert Howarth to allow his photograph to be taken, without realising what the crafty newsman was up to. A few days later the photograph appeared in a national daily newspaper above a caption which read "This is Mr. C.B. James who has reached the rank of Superintendent in the Pembrokeshire Police Force without ever having performed a day's street duty". After that calumnious let-down, Robert Howarth was for many months persona non grata at Goodwick Police Station - and no wonder!

* * * * * *

A local solicitor appearing at Haverfordwest Court to defend a drunk told the magistrates that there were four stages of drunkenness - jocose, verbose, bellicose and comatose. "My client" he claimed optimistically "was approaching the first stage". It didn't work. Fined £5.

* * * * * *

I once saw outside the Wesley Chapel in Pembroke Dock a poster announcing that Mr. William Roblin would be preaching there next Sunday. Immediately below was a Wayside Pulpit message - "Don't Worry, It May Never Happen".

END